GREEN NINJA

Published by J&S Team Summit, Inc
9611 Whitehall Blvd
Spotsylvania, VA 22553

This book is not a substitute for investment advice or professional counseling. The author and publishing company are not responsible for the consequences of the decisions you make after reading this — even if those decisions alter the trajectory of your life in amazing ways.

The author and publishing company have no intent to offend anybody, but cannot anticipate any particular individual's or group's sensitivities. The intent was not to offend, and if you find yourself offended then please complain to a licensed therapist.

The stories presented in this book are unique to the individuals who claim them and are not intended to be duplicated. Their results are not a guarantee of any other individual's results.

Cover design by Aaron Ufema Edited by Caroline P. Smith

Library of Congress Cataloging-in-Publication information:

Larsen, Jim
    Green Ninja: A blueprint to wake the warrior and kick ass at life / by Jim Larsen

ISBN-13: 978-0-9997431-0-2 (softcover : alk. paper)

Dedication:

Jim & Sonya's Team Summit: Without you guys there is no story to tell. I am indebted to you all. Partnering with you, coaching you, and leading you has been one of the most exciting and meaningful journeys of my life.

DailyXperienece: Without you guys there is no book. Your affirmation and passionate response to my coaching content lit a fire in me to pursue this destination. Thank you!

Sadie, Ava, & Haaken: You guys can be anything you want! Dream. Believe. Achieve.

Sonya Beth: You are my heart and soul in the world. Thank you for loving me even on the days it isn't easy!

Table of Contents

Foreword:

The Foundation Supports the Destination

Our bed was never made. Four years ago my wife and I each worked long overnight shifts as registered nurses in hospital settings. We had 3 young kids, and alternated shifts to avoid the headache of finding (and affording) overnight daycare. At 8 a.m., one of us was always just getting home from work. We were getting by but never getting ahead financially. Emotionally, we were dying inside.

We might go 8 days in a row without anything more than passing kids back and forth like ships in the night, stealing a good-bye kiss, and continuing to run full speed ahead without seemingly getting anywhere. Our credit card balance got a little bigger every year, while the savings account we swore we would start never seemed to materialize. We were treading water, and we were living in the shadow of our eventual drowning.

We were desperate to try anything that promised to alter our trajectory. The unlikely answer we found was in the direct selling industry — an industry that sees far more failure than success and can sometimes get a bad rapport for that reason. Our desperation prompted us to try anyway, despite the statistics.

Four years later, our bed is made every morning (Well, most mornings. Okay, we *intend* on making it most mornings!) We have freed ourselves from the grind of running to nowhere. We wake up together, as a family of 5, with an excitement that begs: "What adventure are we going on today?"

We traded drowning for dreaming, and we accomplished it within an industry that churns out more "failure" stories than "success" ones.

In our four years of building a multi-million dollar organization and cultivating a culture of support, encouragement, and celebration, we've had to deal with our share of unfulfilled expectations. While we've coached so many people to amazing places, we've also had people fail to achieve what they wanted to. This book is simply about success and how to go get it.

My passion is to empower people to trade drowning for dreaming, then to establish an intentional plan to go make that dream happen! My driving belief is that you can achieve amazing things, whether you believe that or not. This book offers 7 steps to help you determine what you want from life, and then to go get it so you don't end up drifting 15 years down the road wondering how you got there.

The 7 steps are simple. If you follow them, you'll amaze yourself by what you have accomplished. But I need to introduce a framework for success that I'll refer to often. There are 3 components to every success story:

The Driver: This is you.

The Vehicle: This is your actionable plan to get where you want to go. It might be a school program, it might be a diet or workout regimen, it might be a business model, etc. This is *how* you're going to actually get to your destination.

The Destination: This is where you ultimately want to end up. It's your goal.

While there is an inter-dependence among these three components, they are not equal. Success starts with identifying a destination because you need to have a direction, but the combination of Driver and Vehicle lay the foundation that supports your destination.

It's easy to visualize as a triangle:

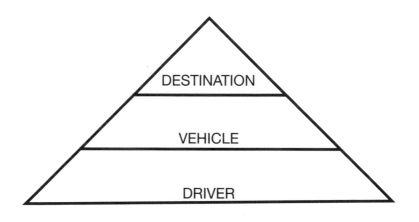

One of biggest reasons people fail to achieve their destination is they fail to build a solid foundation. They may want to achieve big, exciting things, but stacking a big, exciting destination on an insecure foundation never works. The size of your goal is limited to the strength of your foundation to support it.

For example: Let's say the destination you desperately want is a loving, committed marriage relationship. The vehicle you're currently driving is Mike from Karaoke Night at *Applebee's*. And you're the driver.

You don't take Mike to your marriage destination on the first date. You simply don't trust him enough yet to deliver the amazing relationship you envision. You have to get to know Mike a little better. What is he like when he doesn't get what he wants? How does he handle his money? What does he expect from women he dates? Is he ambitious or content to eat chips and watch TV all day?

You'll never take a vehicle to your destination until you trust it, and that trust is always earned over time. Many of us have given up on big dreams because we tied ourselves to a vehicle that we didn't trust.

Sometimes, though, there's nothing wrong with the vehicle. Sometimes the problem is an insecure driver. Mike might be great, but an insecure driver needs validation from everyone else before she can commit. A jaded driver might never truly give Mike a chance to prove himself. A fearful driver might be so afraid of rejection she keeps Mike at an arm's length and never open herself up.

To truly achieve success you have to believe in you. You have to build your confidence and be secure in yourself. Confident drivers make decisions based on what's best for them, whereas insecure drivers make decisions based on what other people think. Confident drivers give a voice to their coaches (the people who believe in them, support them, and celebrate them), whereas insecure drivers give a stronger voice to their critics. Confident drivers are aware of both their strengths and weaknesses while working unapologetically to better themselves. Insecure drivers work too hard to mask their weaknesses to even notice their strengths.

Once you've built your confidence in yourself, choosing a vehicle is easy. A good driver can mask the deficiencies in a lot of vehicles, but it's imperative to believe that the vehicle can get you where you want to go. If you don't trust the vehicle to take you 30 feet down the road, you're not going to trust it to drive you 3,000 miles across the country.

You're going to test drive your vehicle. You're going to give it small goals, and then you're going to hit those goals. You'll raise the bar a little, and then go get it. Each time you "Set goal — hit goal," you're building your belief in both yourself to achieve success and also in the vehicle to get you where you want to go.

Each time you "Set goal — hit goal" you're building the foundation to support a larger and larger destination. Soon, you'll find that your foundation can support dreams that will change the freaking world!

That's the vision behind this book. If you stick with me you'll build your belief in you to achieve amazing things. I cannot wait to hear where it takes you!

Part I

The Destination

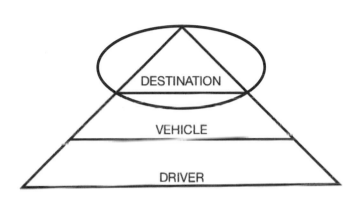

The destination is the start of any success story. Without a destination you cannot move toward a goal because there is no "goal" to move toward. Without a destination you'll float along or you'll spin circles; you'll get caught in the hamster wheel where you can run forever and get nowhere. The destination is the goal, the dream, the vision, the achievement, the reason for doing the hard work. The destination is that thing on the horizon that beckons you.

Chapter I

#KeepingUpWithTheJoneses

"Every morning you have two choices: Continue to sleep with your dreams, or wake up and chase them!" -Unknown author, or lots of authors.

"I am William Wallace! And I see a whole army of my countrymen, here in defiance of tyranny. You've come to fight as free men... and free men you are. What will you do with that freedom? Will you fight? [Against THAT? No. We will run, and we will live!] Aye, fight and you may die. Run, and you'll live... at least a while. And dying in your beds, many years from now, would you be willing to trade all the days, from this day to that, for one chance, just one chance, to come back here and tell our enemies that they may take our lives, but they'll never take... OUR FREEDOM!" -William Wallace, as played by Mel Gibson in Braveheart.

There are always two stories. There's the story we tell publicly. You know the ones: yoga poses bathed in sunlight while we're overlooking the water in our own private oasis. The story of happy children playing peacefully in their multi-layered and perfectly coordinated pastel-colored

8

outfits. The spontaneous date nights with our hot spouses in the private wine cellars of near-forgotten stone mansions.

And then there's the life we actually live: drool-stained pillows, oversleeping snoozed alarms, and wearing yoga pants despite going months without any sort of physical exertion. It's the unexpected chaos when two of your children scream in terror after the third peed on their board game out of protest. It's the exhausted attempt at date night that failed to exceed 8:30pm before fatigue won and you were left with nothing more to show for it than half a Coors Light and Dorito crumbs mixed in chest hair the next morning.

And we tell the public story, because we love the public story. Who wouldn't? It's romantic, it's passionate, it's intentional, it's coordinated. There's order and purpose, excitement, *joie de vivre*, sexiness, and a desirability that is so palpable you've not only accumulated 4,000 followers on your Insta feed, you desperately wish it were real.

There's something so attractive about that story, but it's not just the beauty. There's something deeper about that story that speaks to your soul. There's something about that story that whispers to the core of your very existence with hints and whispers: *"This is what it should be! Do you remember? Do you remember?"*

But we don't remember. And even if we try hard to remember, and even if we catch glimpses of that memory, we're quick to shut it down as a dream and a fantasy. Years ago, there was a little girl. There was a little boy. They dreamt of this life of adventure. Risk. Passion. Beauty.

"My future husband is going to be the handsomest prince in the world."

"I'm going to climb the tallest mountain, and fight the biggest fires."

"I'm going to help other girls believe they're princesses, and they're worth fighting for."

"I'm going to be the best heart doctor in the world."

"I'm going to stop all slavery!"

"I'm going to fight all the bad guys!"

But somewhere along the way, that little girl was taught to stop dreaming and to be realistic. That little boy was taught to settle into a "real" job. All the way back in middle school, our desperation to fit coupled with the terror of standing out, taught us to desire ordinary instead of attracting the attention that comes with extraordinary. We gave up our dreams in order to be "normal". We traded awesome for average — because average doesn't draw attention.

The aesthetic beauty and attraction of the public story we tell isn't desirable for those reasons alone — it's desirable because it reminds the little dreamer in our hearts of what we once had dreamed for. It awakens the child inside us who existed before fear and settling took ownership of our lives. It whispers of what *could have* been. It's nostalgic. And beautiful. And it's not too late.

I've seen this story play out too many times, sadly. And you have, too. That's why I wrote this book, and likely why you're reading it. We dream. We envision. We plan. We expect these amazing lives…and then, out of nowhere, life happens. The demands of school, and work, and marriage, and kids, and work, and kids, and marriage, and business — and we float 10 and 15, maybe even 20 years down the road bouncing from need to need, from demand to demand, until we wake up one day in a panic!

"WHOA! What happened?!? I never would have chosen this for myself! This isn't the job I wanted. This was supposed to just be a stepping stone, and I've been here for 10 years. This isn't the body I wanted. Where did these 40 pounds come from? I never would have picked this for myself. This isn't the relationship I would have chosen to have with my husband. We haven't had sex in 5 months, and neither of us seem to miss it. My kids don't even seem to like me. I never went back to school. I never finished that art project. I never opened that salon. This is not the life I would have chosen — WHAT HAPPENED?!?!"

The vision behind this book is to help you drive your life rather than drift between circumstances. It is to see you fly and not float aimlessly! It is my passion to see you live life by your design and not by your habitual default. The good news, if you're reading this, is that you've likely woken up the

> **"** You've likely been in a mindless slumber that allowed you to float from easy to convenient to comfortable, and never once encouraged you to ask, "But is this what I really WANT!?"

dreamer inside of you! The whisper for something more will begin to grow louder as you continue to shake free from the mindless pattern behaviors that have led you to a life of mediocrity. It's the conscious slumber of settling day in and day out that has made the dreamer inside of you lay comatose for far too long! You've likely been in a mindless slumber that allowed you to float from *easy* to *convenient* to *comfortable*, and never once encouraged you to ask, "But is this what I really WANT!?"

I married up. Seeing pictures of my wife and I together, it becomes immediately apparent that I somehow lucked in to like a two-bucket jump when I got her to agree to marry me. Not one day in our more than 11 years of marriage have I ever taken for granted how lucky I am to wake up with her next to me.

She is the woman who is up early, meditating, fixing lunches for the kids, making the family breakfast, cleaning the house, doing the laundry, going to the gym — the woman who looks so put together from the outside that other women want to be her, and in fairness, other men probably want to be me.

And, of course, the private story is always different than the public one blasted on social media: The other night she was crying on the couch after the kids were in bed. Even after 11 years married, I still don't know how to approach her when she's crying. Does she need space? Does she want me to pry? Should I pretend I didn't notice so I can't be held responsible for whatever reaction I did or did not have? Regardless, I went for it. How could I not!?

She immediately felt embarrassed and guilty for crying, but the reason for her crying was honestly her beautiful awakening. She had been a good kid. A high achiever. Best friends with her mom even through high school. She did what her parents told her. She did what the church told her to do. When she was at school she did what her teachers said. In playing sports she did what her coaches taught. Then she went to college and did what her syllabus told her, and she got a job and did what her boss told her, and got married and did what her husband…haha, let's not get carried away into the world of fiction here, but then she had kids and did anything and everything to delight and appease them. She started a business with me and we did what our mentors told us.

Her faithfulness to living so diligently for other people was rewarded with a financial and time freedom that most people can only dream of. And in that freedom to live, that freedom to dream, that freedom to do anything she wanted — she froze. What did she want? She could do anything, but what was her purpose? Who was she? Thoughts were spinning in her head with no foundation causing her to feel helpless to gain any footing. She had been a good soldier for everyone else for so long, that she simply forgot (or maybe never even knew) herself.

I tell her story because I'm an intimate witness to it, but it's not unique. Maybe the only unique thing is that she positioned herself to wake up in her early 30s, well earlier than a lot of people facing the same dilemma. Many of us have never made a single decision in our lives. We've simply floated from need to need, from crisis to crisis, acting solely on autopilot.

We have all spent years serving the needs of others believing that it's noble and honorable. And sure, at times it was: however, it has also helped us to justify not moving forward with our own lives and dreams. We play the role of the good mom, the good wife, the good husband, the good dad. We're the good son or daughter. We're good to everyone else because it's what's expected of us. It's not only exhausting, worse even, it prevents us from ever stopping to ask if we're being good to ourselves.

We do the laundry every day. We saddle up to a job and a commute we hate. We make meals, and clean up after our kids. We make love to a spouse we may not even really know anymore as if we're robots going through the motions of "should" and "ought". We go to the school that Dad went to so we can pursue the career he wanted us to. We drive 8 hours in the packed mini van with 3 kids through Thanksgiving traffic to visit family that we're not sure we even like because they'd be "disappointed" if we weren't there.

We live and do for others like a good soldier. Like an honorable servant, with little or no regard for ourselves, until we die or we wake up.

My prayer is that you wake up before you die. My hope is that the little dreamer inside you gets a chance to take back your story before it's too late so you can experience what it's like to be free, to live without fear and settling and regret.

Most of us have never made a meaningful choice in our lives, and for some of us, that reality can be crippling. I literally can't take Sonya (my wife) to The Cheesecake Factory because their menu has way too many options — and options are are like headlights to a deer for someone who hasn't claimed their freedom and learned the power of their own choice.

What would your life look like if you lived for you? What would you do if you could do anything? What would you pursue? Who would you be? Where would you spend your holidays if you listened to your own heart instead of your mother's passive aggression? Where would you invest your time? What would you immediately stop doing? Who are you? What do you want? Don't worry if you can't answer these questions — most people have never allowed themselves the freedom to even ask them.

It can be scary! What if, by entertaining these questions, you hurt your mother? Or your husband? Isn't it selfish? Isn't it greedy? Doesn't duty come before self? What if…?

Shhhhhhhhh!

Quiet the noise. You're not trespassing into dangerous territory, you're simply becoming aware of a truth that's always existed. You're free. You're free and you always have been. It's like Dorothy trapped in a dream and desperate to get back to Kansas. After a treacherous and dangerous journey, Glinda, the good witch, lets her know: "You've always had the power to return my dear, you just had to learn it for yourself."

This dutiful life that you have so honorably subjected yourself to is as much a dream as Dorothy's Oz. You've always been free to build your dream, to pursue your passion, to be the best version of you. Every move you make is the result of a choice you have. The freedom you have to move and act, and impose your will.

I got my first tattoo in 2007 in Austin, Texas. I couldn't tell you which studio, or even which neighborhood, or who did it. I can't pretend that it was long thought out, or that I got a range of design pre-approval and affirmation from doting social media followers. It was a tattoo on a whim. Not a drunken whim, but it was spur of the moment nonetheless.

The tattoo was printed on the inside of my right wrist so I could have the word "WILD" staring back at me every time I looked down. It's funny to me to see how people react to it without knowing the backstory. They see the word wild and conjure up imagined stories of nights forgotten in Vegas, time in Mexican jails, and a rebellious unpredictability that is so attractive to some and so unnerving to others.

The truth of the story is far more powerful. That trip to Austin to meet up with a college buddy and groomsman of mine (coincidentally named Austen) was a long time coming. For two years prior, I had been diligently working my first real job — the grown-up kind that comes with a steady salary and health benefits. I think they even had a retirement plan. Before that, I was bartending and waiting tables for tips, spinning circles with a useless bachelor's degree, trying to figure out what I was going to do when I grew up.

I had worked in restaurants since I was 13, originally hired to sweep the parking lot and wash dishes at our local town pizzeria. Restaurants were comfortable for me. But working for cash tips and then spending half my earnings at the bar the same night with my co-workers was getting uncomfortable. The ad in the paper posted by a well-known casual dining chain looking for managers seemed like the perfect fit: the comfort of the restaurant industry, backed by predictable income!

In that first year, I didn't get any paid vacation time, and truth be told, I didn't get any unpaid vacation time either. I simply had to show up. I was allotted six personal days that year, and I saved them all so Sonya and I could go to Mexico for our honeymoon. YES. It's amazing how a steady salary makes you feel so grown up that you can do crazy grown-up things like run off and get married!

In that second year, I got a couple weeks of vacation time, and Sonya was going to be spending a month in Spain with a study abroad program, so it seemed like a perfect opportunity for me to run off for a guy's week and catch up with one of my buddies. I requested to use some of my hard-earned time, but the restaurant was busy and management was short-staffed, so they declined my request.

In frustration, I asked again. And was promptly told no again. When our regional director came to visit the store, I was thrilled! He was instrumental in on-boarding me to the new job, and I had built a good rapport with him. He greeted me warmly, we exchanged some small talk, and then he asked me honestly, "Jim, how's it going in the new location?"

"It's going fine, except, you know Bob, the GM here keeps declining my vacation request, and I sorta feel like I earned the time."

On a dime, with all the scorn and mockery he could muster, he grabbed my arm, pulled me close, stared into my eyes, and I'll never forget this, he says, "Jim, we *own* you!"

I wish I could say that I walked out of there on the spot simply out of principle...but I didn't. I needed the money. We were newly married. Sonya was still in school. I felt chained. I felt enslaved. I felt helpless. I let my fear give his words truth. Out of that fear, I gave up my freedom and showed back up at that job the next day because I had to. It no longer seemed to me that I had a choice.

On reflection, and after some really good Texan margaritas, I realized that they don't own me. I'm wild. You can't cage wild. You can't enslave wild. I own me. And if I show up to work, it's because I choose to. It's because I have determined that it's the best use of my time at the current phase of our life.

I worked that job for 2 more years, but not in bitterness and not out of obligation. I showed up because I chose to. I worked out of freedom and choice. And because I had determined it was worth my time, I gave it my full effort, and I was really really good at it. In their business structure, the kitchen manager (KM) was second in command of the store, behind only the GM. At 25 years old and only 18 months on the job, I was one of the fastest promotions to KM in the company's history.

Had I not realized my freedom, had I not shown up to work out of choice, I would have felt enslaved and taken advantage of. If I had shown up to work everyday with the belief that they didn't deserve me and weren't treating me fairly, I would have naturally slacked off. I would have tried to do less, or seen what I could have gotten away with. I certainly wouldn't have given it my best — because they didn't deserve the best of me.

Only when we realize that nobody is making us sit through traffic to go to that job we hate do we uncover the power of our true freedom and choice. We learn that nobody is forcing us to fold that fourth load of laundry today at the barrel of gun. Our mother doesn't even possess the power to compel us to arrive at her house for Thanksgiving, unless we give her that power.

Battle that traffic and give that job your best because you have decided it is the best means to provide for your family at this phase of life. Fold that laundry with care and pride because you are raising little world changers, and they'll need clean clothes if they're going to change the world. See your mom at Thanksgiving because you choose to, and you want to, and it really isn't that bad.

When you learn to see the world not through the lens of servitude to circumstances beyond your control, but through choices that you're making intentionally, then you have the power to change it. The Apostle Paul wrote a letter to a small Greek church in the first century in which he reminded them that Jesus had set them free from religious rules so that they could be really really free! They needed this reminder because a lot of them were taking their newfound freedom and just choosing to be a slave to the rules again; it was all they knew, and it was comfortable. Isn't that so common for us to do? We have all the freedom in the world, but we give it away out of fear, circumstance, insecurity, doubt, and pretend that we are obligated.

It reminds me of Katy Perry's song *Roar* written by her and Bonnie McKee: "I used to bite my tongue and hold my breath. Scared to rock the boat and make a mess. So I sat quietly. Agreed politely. I guess that I forgot I had a choice. I let you push me past the breaking point. I stood for nothing, so I fell for everything."

You are a better mom when you serve your children out of choice rather than obligation. You can so much better appreciate the little ~~terrors~~ bundles of joy when you position yourself not as their slave, but as their leader! Be the leader who chooses to serve, who chooses to give, who is never taken advantage of or used. They didn't tie you up. They didn't beat you (Well, they probably did, actually. My wife inadvertently gets cracked with a plastic sword almost daily.) And they aren't forcing you to obey their whim.

You are a better employee when you arrive to work on time and give that job all of your talent and creative energy because you've chosen to be there. You are honest. You are hardworking. You are talented. But if you approach that job like the boss owns you, or is taking advantage of you then you'll be bitter. When you're bitter, you won't give it your best. When you don't perform your best, you won't earn the promotion. Be there because you choose to be there. Do your best because you decided, all on your own, that this was the best use of your time today. And if it isn't the best use of your time, quit. Life is too short to pursue someone else's dream!

Your husband doesn't want you making love to him out of obligation to some antiquated "duty." Your children don't want you growing bitter toward them while you clear the dinner table. Your boss doesn't want an employee who'd rather jump off a bridge than turn in expense reports. Whatever you do, wherever you are, realize it's your choice, and if you've chosen it — own it. If it's worth your time, give it your effort!

Time is the single resource we cannot replace. A lot of us have given years of our time that we can never get back, pursuing someone else's dream, living lives that someone else wanted us to live. We worked jobs we never liked. We avoided pursuing opportunities because we worried what people would think. At worst, we're doing things we hate for people we don't like because we're supposed to and we're taught to keep up with the Joneses, and at best, we do things that are good, for people we love, but often out of a sense of duty and obligation rather than grace and freedom.

We are free. You are free. The life you're living is the life you've chosen. Own your choices. The minute we take responsibility for everything, we have the power to change anything. But too often, we use our freedom to subject ourselves to bondage. We do chores because we think we *have* to, when in reality, we don't! We could hire someone to do that laundry. We could live in dirty clothes. We could teach the kids to do it themselves. Nobody is going to die today if that laundry doesn't get folded. You aren't doing it because you have to. You do it because you choose to.

You have the freedom. You have the power. You can awaken that dreamer, take back your story and kick ass at life!

The purpose of this chapter is to help you realize that you always have a choice, and that the reality you experience everyday and call your life can be chosen, designed, and intentional rather than just a thoughtless piece of driftwood being carried by a current to nowhere special.

Let's instead go somewhere special. But to do that, we're going to have fight the current. And that's not always going to be easy, especially if you've done nothing but drift with the current since you first learned to be obedient to your parents. There will be tears. Maybe ugly tears. There will be precious comfort zones that will fight like heck to stay intact and keep you safely warm inside of their fuzzy, complacent embrace. You will have some friends who will likely judge you, or unfriend you on Facebook because your newfound vision is rocking the boat that you've all been floating in together for awhile, and they prefer the soothing ride, gentle breeze, and mindless current that has kept them warmly embraced on their trip to nowhere special for so long.

They'll yell: "SIT DOWN! Stop rocking the boat! We have it good here!" And sadly, some of you will probably listen to them. You've gotten good at listening to them over the years, and it isn't easy to all of a sudden stand up, rock the damn boat, and then even jump out and start swimming upstream if it comes to that. I got to a point where I was so desperate, I think I even yelled an imaginary "CANNONBALL!" as I bailed out and soaked the people I had to leave behind.

But honestly, until it comes to that, you're probably not ready. Which brings me to the first major key to success that we have to uncover. In order to be successful, you have to want something, and it has to be something that really excites you. Tony Robbins says it this way: "People are not lazy, they just have impotent goals: that is, goals that do not inspire them."

For example: You're a starving artist in the city who really wants to make it big! You have small, regular gigs, a couple nights a week, and you locked down the corner of the park where the Metro lets out on weekends, which is awesome, because you've been eyeing that corner forever but it was always Duncan's corner until his very convenient arrest left a void that you quickly jumped to fill. And you haven't really crossed the bridge concerning what happens when Duncan gets out...but that'll figure itself out later.

For now? It's yours. You're good. Rent is paid. Sometimes it's even paid on time. You've got a circle of amazing friends who are all fighting like you to nail down their gigs, while bartending, working at Starbucks, and the one guy who actually owns a car in the city drives for Uber.

This is your boat. It's drifting. You're 38 years old, and you moved to the city to "make it" 13 years ago. You're surrounded by people who look like you, talk like you, and are pursuing the same dream that you are, with the same lack of any real or actual positive trajectory toward achieving it.

This is where you have a choice — continue for the next 13 years, doing what you've been doing. Or muster up all the courage you have, stand up, and jump out of the damn boat. Maybe that looks like scraping the money together to record an actual demo, creating a professional LinkedIn account, putting on some clothes that were washed within the last week, and forcing your way into an audience with the managers of the best clubs in Mid Town.

None of that is comfortable. And at first, you're probably gonna suck at it. You'll risk losing your corner of the park and your friends will think you've "sold out," especially when they see you leave the apartment in clean clothes. And you're going to wonder every single day if it's really worth it.

For most people, it isn't worth it. It's not that they're lazy, as Tony says, it's just that "making it" as a performer is an impotent goal. It doesn't really excite them, and it's not worth the cost of their comfort zone.

If you're going to achieve something, if you're going to be successful, if you're going to kick ass at life, you're going to have to jump out of that boat. But in order to have the courage to even stand up in the boat, you need to want something. And you need to want it with all the gusto and determination of a chubby kid at a pie-eating contest.

Steve Tobak is a rock-star tech executive, author, and leadership coach. He wrote a great article, and it was too good to just paraphrase:

[Successful people] always wanted more out of life, so they always strove to achieve more…Sure, they also had the guts to take risks, but that's really no different from being willing to get on a really scary ride at the amusement park.

Just think about it. If you go to the amusement park and you're only willing to go on the boring rides, you can sort of sleepwalk your way through the whole thing. Then when nighttime comes, you wonder what all the hoopla was about. But if, on the other hand, you challenge yourself, face your fear, and get on those terrifying rides, you'll end up with loads of wonderful memories of an eventful and fulfilling day.

Life is the same way…If you're content with who and what you are, that's great. Stick with it and call it a day. If you're not, the message here is a simple one. Keep getting on those rides until you've had your fill. Then, when nighttime falls, I guarantee you'll feel like you've had one hell of a fun day at the amusement park.

You will never find the courage or motivation to stand up for something that you don't want. You will never rock the boat for something that isn't very exciting. You won't swim against the current if you have no idea where you're swimming to. So you have to want something, and you have to ask yourself: "Am I willing to disrupt my routine, in all of its comfortable glory, to achieve this?" If the answer is yes, you just might be ready to kick ass at life.

And if you're just not sure what you want, or where you're going, or what your purpose is, or what God's called you to — that's okay. Sometimes it's just enough to want out of the boat with the faith and belief that the next steps will reveal themselves as soon as you show the courage to move.

Maybe you think you know what you want, and if that's the case, I want to offer a word of warning: it's probably deeper than you're imagining. Often the things we think we want are simply results of the action we take, they aren't the goal.

For example: we think we want to lose weight, when in reality, losing weight isn't very exciting, it's arbitrary. What we actually want is to feel sexy, or to have our spouse desire us, or to catch the eye of the bartender, or to fit into that knockout dress, etc…

We might think our goal is to make a million dollars. What we actually want, however, is to feel successful, and accomplished. What we really desire is to get out of debt, build that dream house, or feel free to pursue the exciting things and opportunities that a surplus of money allows. Maybe what we really want is our father to be proud of us or for our neighbor to admire us. Nobody accumulates money simply to have a bigger bank account.

There's a story of a contractor with grown children who poured every spare minute he had into building his own personal dream house. He literally dreamt of this house. He poured his savings into building it. He talked constantly of it. This was his dream, his baby, his mission. It was the thing he wanted.

Only when he was asked "*why*" he wanted that house, did he come to truly understand his heart. When he was asked why he wanted this house so badly, he paused and replied, "Well, honestly, I've worked so hard my whole life that I've missed out on so much. I missed my kids growing up. I missed my friends. I want to build this house so that when I retire I have a place to entertain and have parties. I want a place that people will want to come to and then I won't miss out anymore."

"Well, why don't you want to miss out on things?"

"I guess because I realize now that life is short. The kids grew up so fast. I always thought I'd have more time. I feel guilty for missing some of the most important moments with my kids because of seemingly insignificant moments at work."

"So what you're saying is that time with your kids is the most important thing in the world, but you're spending your time working to build a house."

The man stopped construction, sold the house, bought an RV, and now travels between his kids' homes. He thought he knew what he wanted until he was asked why.

An impotent goal won't provide the drive necessary to overcome the obstacles that will inevitably arise. So if you're still thinking in terms of a quantifiable goal, ask yourself why. Then ask why again. And again. This will un-peel the layers until you're left with what your heart truly wants out of this life.

Once the layers are unpeeled, and you're staring deeply at the thing you most want in this life, it's going to feel so far away! You're going to wonder if you'll ever get there. You're furthermore going to have no idea how to get there. That's also okay. All we need to start is an exciting destination that you're willing to get uncomfortable for in order to achieve. Once you have that exciting thing in mind, make a vision board so you can physically see it in front of you. Chasing a goal you can see is a lot easier than an imaginary one in your head.

Over the next few chapters we're going to work of the 'how' stuff out and it's going to be fun. I promise!

Step I is simple:

"Want something."

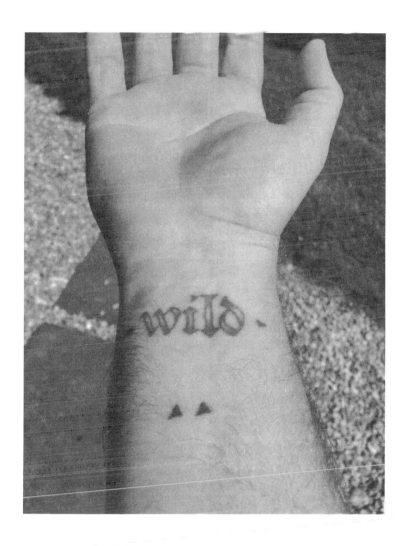

Post Chapter Questionnaire:

Question 1: Are there things you do day in and day out because you feel like you "have to" or you're "obligated" or you don't have a choice? Reframe those in your mind with intentional language. Instead of thinking: "I have to fold laundry today," say out loud, "I choose to fold laundry." Replace the "have to" or the "obligation" with the words choice "CHOOSE TO". Write it down and say it out loud to remind yourself of your freedom and choice. You'll be amazed how the words that come out of your mouth frame your mind and determine your attitude about what you're doing. There's a switch that flips in our mind when we realize we're acting out of choice instead of obligation.

Question 2: What does your perfect day look like?

Question 3: What would you do this week, this year, for the next 5 years, if there were no variables (i.e., don't think about money, kids, bills, qualifications, location, etc.) except the excitement in your heart?

Now, I realize that when you're financially or emotionally drowning, you're not in a position to dream. I know this, because I've been there. You have to get your feet on solid ground, because the only thing you can think of when you're drowning is catching that next breath. So, when we're talking about wanting something, maybe you haven't had the time, space, or freedom to think through the first two questions. That's okay. We need to get your feet back on solid ground first.

So if that describes you, understand that wanting something doesn't have to be the big, giant, passionate reason you were placed on this green earth. To start, you just have to want something that's big enough and exciting enough to get you off the couch, but not so big that it overwhelms you.

I see people make both of these mistakes often. The first mistake happens when the thing they want isn't very exciting. They don't need it. They kind of want it, but they don't want it more than they want to watch *American Ninja Warrior* with a cold beer. That level of wanting something isn't going to inspire action. It's the "impotent goal" that Tony talks about.

The other mistake happens when people set a goal that is so far beyond their ability to envision or believe. It's not that the goal is unrealistic or impossible — it might be an amazing goal! Maybe the goal is to build 30 orphanages in the poorest countries of the world. That's amazing! And exciting! But also overwhelming for someone who hasn't learned to believe in themselves. They start down the road, and 6 months in, when they're still miles away, they lose heart and give up.

To start, just picture something that is super exciting to you, but not overwhelming. Here are some questions that will help you:

Question 4: Is anything causing you so much stress that you can't get yourself to see the dreams that live on the other side of it? (Is it $15,000 in credit card debt? Is it a job that's sucking the life from you? Is it a house you can't afford? Is it a child who is making bad decisions?)

Question 5: What do you want? What is that thing that's exciting enough to get you off the couch and out of your routine, but not so big that it overwhelms you? Why do you want it? Why?

The answer to question 5 is important. It's actually everything. If you don't want something, you won't work for it, and it won't happen. It's the foundation. But I phrase the question carefully, because while there is no limit to how big that thing is (Literally you can write $10 million, or a 10,000-square-foot house outside of San Fransisco, etc.), but as you'll learn in later chapters, your dream can't be bigger than your belief in yourself. Sometimes we need to build our belief by achieving smaller goals first. Other times, we just need the permission and green light to get our dream on paper.

Question 6: If the thing you answered in Question 5 could be yours, how much effort would that be worth?

Part II

The Driver

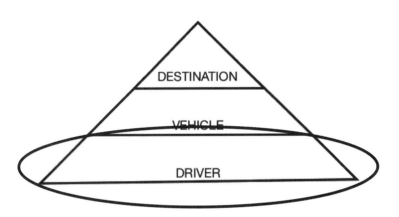

The driver is by far the most important component in any success story, and it is often the most overlooked. We're taught to have a goal and learn how to go get it.

Unfortunately, determining a goal and then understanding how to go get it often doesn't equate to actual results at all. The world is full of people who know where they'd like to go and have an amazing destination in mind. Many of these people also know exactly what to do in order to achieve that goal, and yet they cannot get themselves to actually put one foot in front of the other and make it happen. It's often not a lack of knowledge that prevents people from hitting goals. It's often a lack of confidence or a lack of feeling worthy.

See the difference between a confident driver and an insecure one:

Insecure Driver	Confident Driver
• Needs validation from others to affirm their decisions	• Makes decisions based on what's best for them
• Gives more power to their critics than their coaches	• Gives more power to their coaches than their critics
• Blames others (including the vehicle) for their failure	• Takes responsibility for their results
• Focused on hiding their weaknesses, while often unaware of their strengths	• Confidently embraces both their strengths and weaknesses while working unapologetically to better themselves

If you don't believe in your ability to arrive at the destination, then knowing how to get there doesn't matter at all! To achieve success, you need to build your belief in you!

Chapter II:

#TheSweatPantsMaster

"Whether you think you can or think you can't, you're right." -Henry Ford, American Car maker, dreamer and do-er of the impossible.

"You are what you believe yourself to be." -Paulo Coelho de Souza, a Brazilian writer with the largest social media following in the entire world.

There are three variables necessary to achieve any goal but they're not equal. You can't just divide the pie chart in three even pieces and talk about them equally. They're layered and intertwined. They're each important but at varying levels.

In the last chapter we talked about one of them: the goal, the destination, the thing you want. While that's absolutely necessary because it sets the course and the direction, it's powerless to actually get you there.

People don't get rich, run marathons, or play Rachmaninoff's Prelude in G Minor on the piano just because they want to. Achievement doesn't happen by wanting. Wanting just sets the destination. To get there you need a vehicle and driver. It's the three fold marriage of driver, vehicle, and destination that determine anyone's success.

The vehicle is the actual methodology you employ day in and day out. If your destination is getting sexy for the beach, the vehicle is the gym, or the trainer, or the diet program. The vehicle is the actionable plan.

You are the driver and I'm going to propose, as I mentioned earlier, that this is not a pie chart split three ways evenly. By far the most important variable is the driver. It's you. Companies that offer vehicles (programs to achieve goals) want you to believe that anyone can succeed because of their vehicle. It's a lie. For every success story in a MLM, diet program, study guide, etc., there are hundreds of failure stories.

The people that successfully drive any vehicle to their destination did it because they were an amazing driver! They succeeded because they showed up and actually put the plan into action. The vehicle is important, but far less than the driver. The person that was successful with one diet program likely would have been successful with another. It wasn't the program or the vehicle that determined their success — it was them.

A good driver can handle almost any vehicle, and perhaps most importantly can identify the vehicle they'd be best suited to drive. A good driver can trouble-shoot when things are going wrong and they can find detours around obstacles. When the driver believes in themselves, there is almost no vehicle that won't work for them.

One of the flaws of success coaching today is the intense focus on the goal and the method, vanquishing the individual to nothing but an after-thought. There are endless diet programs that show you pictures of success stories (the goal or destination), and introduce you to their supplement, or workout program (the vehicle), and that's it. For most of us, knowing where we want to go, and even knowing how to get there, just doesn't seem to be enough to actually get us moving.

It's often not a lack of knowledge that keeps us stuck. In order to put a plan into action, a driver has to be unashamedly confident in their self. When a person is secure in their giftedness while recognizing their weaknesses; confident in their ability and not insecure; when he or she can make commitments and stick with them, make decisions and own the consequences; when they can act boldly and intentionally — then that person will be successful in any endeavor they pursue. A good driver will get to their destination! We start with "wanting something" because we need to have a direction, but it's imperative that we skip how to get there for now because far more important than 'how' is 'who'.

The next handful of chapters will explain this further.

MTV was the only best hope. And I wasn't allowed to watch it. Not only was it purportedly made by the devil and designed intentionally to get teenagers to have sex, but also, we couldn't afford it. Like we couldn't afford anything we wanted. That was a frequent theme throughout my childhood.

I'll never forget the day I walked up Main Street to the school yard playground to play basketball and my friend, Andrew, was there waiting for me with his brand new Reebok pumps. YES! You could actually increase the pressure on the sides of your feet simply by repeatedly pressing this half-sphere bubble on the tongue of the shoe painted to look like a basketball. I don't think anyone ever figured out why someone would want to do this...but it was cool. I mean, before we started playing, he made sure to yell "TIME OUT" so everyone could watch him bend over and pump them up. And yes, there was a "pressure release valve" also built in — I mean, they thought of everything!

Within a week, all the guys we played with were calling intermittent time outs to adjust the pressure of their shoes. All except for me of course. I got my shoes from Ames — which was basically a discount store that Wal-Mart sent their discontinued stuff to. There was nothing sexy about Ames, or their shoes, or the people who shopped there, or me, for that matter. An older brother would have been a really helpful tool at this point in my life, but my parents didn't give me one of those, either.

So without an older brother, MTV was really my only hope at differentiating between "cool" and "un-cool." I mean, these were the '90s. There was no internet so I certainly couldn't jump on YouTube or a Pinterest fashion board to get fashion advice. I didn't know how to be "cool" or who could teach me!

My parents were no help, either, when it came to this. My mom was not the one who aimed for us to look like the Abercrombie Kids catalogue, despite my pleadings. Rather, she was valedictorian of both her high school and college classes. She was even the top student in her medical school class when she decided to quit in order to start a family. She was far more concerned with things like making sure we knew how to read and write and handle basic arithmetic without a calculator. If she could have afforded a bumper sticker, it probably would have read, "I gave my kid the genetics to achieve honor roll, and can't figure out why no one can tell."

My dad was a workaholic. He earned a master's degree in theology and moved his family of five to a small town in rural New England to pastor an old church that had 35 members and paid him $12,000 a year. We lived in a 2-

bedroom, 1-bathroom house that the church owned, and shockingly, a cable subscription was not in the budget.

There was always Andrew, though! We had an unspoken trade agreement: He could eat all the sugary breakfast cereal his mom forbade when he was at our house, and I got full control of the TV remote at his. Of course, that meant MTV music videos during the day and *Beavis and Butthead* at night.

Apparently, those intermittent connections to a bigger, wider world weren't enough, though, because I was bullied. Some of it was my own fault, I suppose, or maybe that's just what the bullies made me believe; nonetheless, I was dubbed: the "Sweat Pants Master." And the bullies further insisted that I was so fat I sweat Crisco. They later changed that to bacon grease, and eventually just started calling me "Bacon." Like any kid in school, I desperately wanted to be liked. I wanted to fit in and get invited to birthday parties, but totally would have settled for even just a seat at a cafeteria lunch table.

Of all the bullying though, the hardest for me to swallow was the "Sweat Pants Master." On the surface, it was really pretty simple: I wore sweat pants to school every day. Literally, EVERY. SINGLE. DAY. My brother and I liked to play "ninja" at home, and clearly ninjas wore solid colors. Hence, we made every effort to match our sweat pants with our sweat shirts. We even developed an entire

43

hierarchy color system to determine which color dominated which other color. There was no question that if I was wearing solid black then I had to win. Using our color coded chart: White was the wimpiest, then red, then blue, then green, then black wins all! Looking back, we never wore the same color at the same time, and to this day, I'm not sure how we'd resolve a tie-breaker.

That gentle/semi-violent naïveté worked fine in the insular world of our home; however, as I'm sure you can imagine, it didn't translate well to our school. I'd show up to school in a solid green sweatsuit for like the third day in a row — obviously still dressed as a Green Ninja — and I'd get called the "Sweat Pants Master." I didn't like that name, and upon further introspection, I cannot gather:

1. Why didn't I just wear something different after clearly noting the correlation between the name I didn't like and the clothing I was wearing?

2. Why did my mom let me leave the house for the three days strong as the Green Ninja? I mean, I get that we couldn't afford for me a model at the Gap, but there could have been some middle ground, right!?

Regardless, after Green Ninja day three in the sixth grade, someone called me out on the fact that I hadn't changed my clothes, and for some reason, that was the first time it entered my head that "HOLY CRAP! He's RIGHT! I haven't changed my clothes in 3 days!?" Suddenly, I was embarrassed for so many reasons! Obviously, I was embarrassed for being called out publicly, but internally, I started wondering: "What's wrong with me? How did I not notice this?"

Embarrassment does funny things to us, doesn't it? It causes us to want to run, hide, lie, or die — practically anything to disappear in that moment. So I did what any kid would do: I made up a possible but absolutely improbable story and I stuck to it, hard.

"Oh, I changed my clothes. When I got home from school, I took this off and threw it in the washer, and wore something else. That way, I could wear the same thing to school, and it would be clean."

I mean, sure. That's possible. But no, my mother was not washing a single outfit so I could wear it again, and there was no way I was doing my own laundry. Meaning, this scenario would have never ever actually played out, but I stuck with it because my honor, my ego, and my sixth grade reputation depended on it. It was short-lived as they all saw right through it anyway.

Over the years, I've asked my mother about it. With the kind and gentle spirit she is, she's so graciously answered, "Jim, you insisted it was comfortable, and I didn't feel like fighting you."

What had been brewing for some time came to a head one fall evening. It was the first school dance of the year, and as a sixth grader, it was my first school dance ever. I could barely contain my excitement! We had been watching the middle schoolers go to school dances for the last couple years, and it was finally our turn! Everyone was going to be there. The music was going to be loud. The lights were going to be low. The student-to-adult ratio would be so very much in our favor. I mean, this was our night. This was *my* night.

Everything had to be perfect! This was my chance to be cool. The other kids might not like me during school hours, but this was different. This was almost like "outside of school." It was like I was invited to the party. I had to make a good impression!

So I picked red. It wasn't very high up on the color chart that hung on the back of our shared bedroom door, but it was clean and it matched the colors in my Tasmanian Devil tie, which I was certain would put me in good with the cool kids. I slipped the pre-tied tie over my head (thanks Dad!), left it loose because, well, my red sweatshirt didn't really have a collar anyway, kissed my mom, and ran out the door.

We lived close enough to the school that I could walk there, so that night, I even ran the whole way. I was on Cloud 9. This was *my* night. And walking in, it was everything I expected it to be. The music was loud. The lights were low. Britt was even there! She was the prettiest girl in school. The one who everyone wanted to dance with, be with, laugh with, especially be seen with! Britt's presence automatically meant this was the coolest place to be, and I was there. I was in the coolest place, basically hanging out with Britt. Totally #WINNING.

And that's when I heard it. "Hey Sweat Pants Master, this is a school dance, haven't you ever heard of jeans?"

Yeah, yeah, I had heard of jeans. Why didn't I just wear jeans? I probably owned jeans. It wouldn't have even been hard to put jeans on. Is that what cool people wore? Why hadn't I ever just paid attention to what other kids were wearing? Did he at least notice my Taz tie?

"Hey Sweat Pants Master, come here!" I didn't want to go there. But they were the cool kids. What choice did I really have?

"Hey Sweat Pants Master, COME HERE!"

They were standing next to the stage where the DJ was set up. I was scared. All of a sudden the loud music, the low lights, and the high student-to-adult ratio that had so excited me earlier were all of a sudden not in my favor. I bounced nervously over to them, trying not to expose my fear.

"Hey Sweat Pants Master, we wanna show you something outside."

Really? What's outside? I mean what could be outside that you'd wanna show me? It's dark out. It seems like all the fun is in here. Can't we stay in here? Isn't there anything in here you wanna show me?

They surrounded me. Four of them. All in eighth grade. And they escorted me down the service hallway and out the side door. I knew this wasn't going to go well, but I felt powerless to effect any change. I didn't know what to do or what to say, so I went along for the ride, which brought me out the door, had me bear hugged and lifted by the other 3, and dropped down into the dumpster.

I heard the snickering. I heard the high fives. I climbed out.

I wasn't done. This was *my* night. I couldn't let one little mishap ruin this magical moment that was surely going to change the trajectory of everything for me. So I brushed myself off. Took a whiff to make sure I wasn't repulsive, and I walked right back into that service door. And they were right there.

Why didn't I wait longer for them to assimilate into a larger crowd, or find something else to do? Why did I have to be so damn efficient and determined to go back in so quickly?

They were efficient, too. Literally wasting no time, they escorted me back outside, and tossed me into the trash heap a second time.

I climbed out. I brushed myself off. And this time, I just walked home. And I remember thinking as I walked home, "I'm AWESOME! They just don't know it yet."

How does that happen? How does a single sharp comment destroy the ego of some, and yet an experience like this can't touch the ego of others?

How would you have responded to this? How would your kids respond? I've been forced to look back and ask, "Why? How did I know this? How was I so unscathed?"

The answer comes from my dad. I mentioned he was a workaholic. He had to be stressed. He was fully supporting a family of five on a meager salary, and he worked to earn it. A lot. Often 14-hour days, often 7 days a week. He didn't know my friends' names. He didn't know what I was learning in school. I'm not even sure he could have told you what grade I was in. But that stuff was irrelevant to him. It was far more important to him that I knew who I was, and he told me who I was:

"Jim, you are bold, and independent, and you're going to make a strong stand for God."

"Jim, you are bold, and independent, and powerful."

"Jim, what are you?"

"I'm bold, I'm independent, and powerful. I'm going to make a strong stand for God."

I didn't even know what any of that even meant. But I could repeat it. I could repeat it in my sleep. He had been telling me this since my earliest memories. He'd make me repeat it to him, over and over, and over — until it was annoying.

"Jim, what are you?"

Cue the eye roll. "Seriously, Dad? We're doing this again? I'm in middle school now. I know what I am: I'm bold. I'm independent. I'm powerful."

I. KNOW. WHAT. I. AM.

I didn't know it at the time, but he was speaking life and truth and destiny into my heart. He repeated it ad nauseam so it would stick. So it would sink into the very core of my understanding of self.

"I know what I am."

As a result, there was no question in my mind. I knew who I was. And I knew that climbing out of that dumpster on that cool fall evening didn't look bold, or independent, or powerful, but I also knew that moment in time didn't determine my destiny. It was just a snapshot on a timeline of power and courage. I was going places. They couldn't stop me. I was awesome. They just didn't know it yet.

———————————————

There are always two stories. There's the story we tell people, and then there's the story our hearts whisper to us in the dark. There's our public story, the one we tell our kids and our neighbors, and holiday guests. And there's our private story — the one we really believe about ourselves.

That private story is the one that whispers to us when no one else is around. The one that speaks to us when we look in the mirror, or try on the jeans, or wonder if we'd succeed at that business or that project. It's the one that influences whether we go for it or play it safe. It's the story we tell ourselves that determines if we put ourselves out there or shrink back.

What is the private story that your heart whispers to you? Is it one of doubt? Insecurity? Bad circumstance? Is it a story of power? Confidence? Overcoming?

My dad gave my heart a story before outside influences had a chance to infiltrate it with lies. The world wanted me to believe that I was fat, ugly, friendless, worthless — and I likely would have. Except I already had a story. By the time others tried to sell me a bad story, I already had a story of power, of purpose, of independence, and because my heart whispered that story to me, there was no circumstance that could define my reality, no matter how ugly, boisterous, and difficult it was.

It gets better! The best part in all this is that if you're unhappy with your story, it's not too late to change it! We've talked about how it's imperative to know what you want, but knowing that is pointless if you don't believe that you're powerful and able to make it your reality. The destination you desperately want to arrive at will never happen if you don't believe you're capable of getting there!

_____

If you don't get anything else out of this chapter, get this: Life isn't going to be friendly or kind to us, especially if we choose to rock the boat. If you choose to truly stand up and go for it, you need to be ready to fall flat on your face while walking down stairs, in a tuxedo, at a party you felt totally unqualified to be invited to. And the people you were so hoping to impress are instead going to laugh before they even check to see if you're okay.

If you are not dead set on who you are and where you're going, then the obstacles are going to be too hard to overcome. With each new challenge, you're going to renew the question: Is this really worth it? And eventually, if you are not absolutely certain about the inevitability of your success, then the answer one day will be "NO." If you are not absolutely certain about the inevitability of your success, then you are simply waiting for the obstacle that will ultimately derail you.

Let me illustrate the power of belief. In 1957, Curt Richter did an experiment on rats. Now, I don't in any way condone cruelty to animals, I happen to love animals. So I'm not sharing this story to be shocking or crude but rather to illustrate the phenomenal.

Curt was curious one day, apparently, to learn how long rats could swim before drowning. I don't know what sparked his curiosity, but it didn't seem like a hard experiment to set up: Get a container. Fill it with water. Put some rats in it. Set a timer.

After about 15 minutes, there was no movement left in that container. So the answer to his burning question was: Rats can swim for 15 minutes before drowning. If it ever pops up on *Jeopardy*, you are now armed with a piece of otherwise useless trivia.

But Curt wasn't done. He set the whole thing up again. Container, water, rats, timer. But this time, just before the 15 minute mark when the rats were going to expire, he saved them! He took them out, he dried them off, he put them back in their warm, cozy homes. And probably fed them cheese balls stuffed with peanut butter for their trouble.

The last part of his experiment involved doubling everything. Two containers, both filled with water, a lot of rats, and a couple of stop watches. In one container he placed a new batch of rats, and they began swimming literally for dear life. In the other container, he placed that group of previously saved rats, and they began swimming. The question was simple: Would the previously saved rats outperform their counterparts?

The new batch of rats performed exactly as expected. Fifteen or so minutes. No movement left. Make the note on the results pad. Scoop out the soggy, hairy bodies (BLEH!). Check in on the other rats.

Well, the other rats seemed to still be going strong. But for how long? Would they outperform their peers by 15 percent and swim for more than 17 minutes? They couldn't double the performance of their peers and swim for half an hour, could they? I mean, I don't even think I can swim for half an hour!

They didn't swim for half an hour. That group of previously saved rats swam for more than 60 hours! They swam for days! D A Y S!!!!! They didn't simply outperform their peers, they blew their peers out of the water by 24,000 percent. They swam 240 times longer than their counterparts because they had been there before and they knew they were going to be saved.

The 15-minute rats didn't know how the story was going to end. They panicked. They fought. And with no hope, and no story of a better tomorrow, they gave up. It's easy. It's easy to give up when we aren't sure if it's ever going to get better. It's easy to give up if our success isn't inevitable. We fight for as long as it seems worth it, and then we let go.

But the rats that swam for days, while they were facing the same obstacle as their friends, they had hope. They had a story that told them: "If I just hang on a little longer, things are going to start looking up!"

> It isn't that successful people had a smooth road and didn't face obstacles. It's that they were empowered with a story that made their obstacles irrelevant.

"If I just keep going, that peanut butter cheese ball is going to taste all the better."

"I know this looks bad, and it is bad, but I'm getting out of here. I'm moving forward. My story is much bigger than this pot!"

It isn't that successful people had a smooth road and didn't face obstacles. It's that they were empowered with a story that made their obstacles irrelevant. There are people, walking around today who are outperforming their peers by 24,000 percent, and you can be one of them, too! But you have to believe that your success is inevitable! That your day is coming! That you are a badass who is going to take over your little corner of the world.

This belief doesn't come naturally for a lot of us. We're born into this world as blank, wide-eyed slates who are just taking everything in. Wonder. Magic. Awesomeness. But as soon as we can form memories, we start hearing "chubby," "not good enough," "not smart," "not pretty," "can't kick the ball," "too slow," "smells bad," "dirty," "freckle face," "four-eyes" and these examples are benign compared to the ones that strike at the core of our identity: "nigger," "faggot," or "retard."

These words give us a lens, and we start seeing the world through that lens. "Dad spends a lot of time at work, and when he gets home, he doesn't have much time for me. It must be because I'm (fill in the blank with the words you heard that you started believing)." Or, "my sister is really good at gymnastics, and I can't do half the stuff she can. It must be because I'm _____." "How did I forget to turn that assignment in? It must be because I'm _____." "I didn't make the basketball team, it must be because I'm _____"

Then, once the lens is properly fit and we're interpreting our experiences through it, we go further and we start projecting the lens onto future potential experiences: "She would never want to go out with me because I'm _____." "I could never get that job because I'm _____." "Just because they did it, doesn't mean I can do it, because I'm _____"

It goes a little like this:

1. Hear the words.

2. Believe the words

3. Interpret the behaviors of others and self through the lens of the words.

4. Project the words onto future actions.

From the time I have memories, my Dad told me I was bold, and independent, and powerful. I believed those words. I had no reason not to. So I started interpreting the world through those words which looked a lot like this:

"Hmm…they didn't choose me for the kickball team. No worries, I'm bold and independent, so I'll go play basketball instead." "My dad is really busy, and doesn't seem to have time for me, but it must just be his job, because who wouldn't want to spend time with me?" "I just got thrown in a dumpster at my first school dance, but that's okay, I can rent a movie on my way home."

Then I started projecting those words onto future actions which propelled me forward: "That girl is stunningly beautiful, and everyone wants to talk to her. She must be amazing. I'm bold, so I'll gladly go talk to her!" "The chances of getting that job are so small, but I have to at least try. I'm powerful, so I expect they'll see that in the interview!" "What will people think if I join that direct selling company? I don't care. I'm independent and it looks like an amazing opportunity; I'm going to go for it!"

The words you believe influence how you see the world and determine whether you'll take chances and move forward or not risk it and stay stuck. And maybe you have some really sucky words that have been holding you back for so long. Maybe you believe really small things about yourself.

And I hate that for you, but I also know it's not too late to change it!

To be honest, I don't think you can afford not to change it! You have to if you want to be successful! It isn't just enough to want something. You have to believe that you can and will achieve it. From here on, you're going to start giving yourself some new words. They will be life-giving words. They will be brave and bold, and sexy, and risky and powerful words. You're going to write them on sticky notes, or have them printed on 5-foot canvasses and placed all around your house. You're going to see your words of life staring back at you from the bathroom mirror when you brush your teeth. You're going to see them on the refrigerator when you go for your third serving of ice cream. You're going to see them on the TV remote when you're switching channels, and on the computer screen, and as the wallpaper on your phone.

Here's one thing to expect: It's going to feel weird. You're going to feel like an imposter. It's going to feel fake, and artificial, and extremely awkward: especially when the neighbor comes over to pick up that piece of mail she's been meaning to grab since last month and notices your sticky notes. But you know what? You no longer care what she thinks. You're doing this for you because you need it.

Here are some examples. You can take them and use them or make up your own. And one really good idea is to have someone you love, trust, and respect make a few for you. Especially at first, it seems more valid when it comes from someone else:

"My purpose will be fulfilled."

"I am not finished."

"I can do anything."

"I am loved."

"Progress over perfection."

"What I say is important."

"I am beautiful."

"I am confident."

"I will win."

"I am sexy as hell, and this dress has never looked better on anyone!"

"I am enough."

It's not enough to just read them. Say them out loud. Say them loudly, with your hands in the air in a power pose. Believe it. Rise above. You were once a baby, taking it all in, and you just heard the wrong words, but it's time for new words!

And if you're a parent, I hope you start giving your children words like my dad gave me. Until we had our son four years ago, I spent five years as a dad of daughters. We have two girls. I knew that the world today is even harder on girls than it was when I was growing up. Between music, magazines, the internet, TV shows, movies... we are inundated to believe that women are nothing more than pleasure toys for boys.

I knew my girls would be sold the lie that they are dumb, ugly, and weak. So from the day they were born, I gave them different words. I told them that they are beautiful, and strong, and smart! I make them repeat it to me every day. Before school, they climb on top of the kitchen chairs, raise their arms up like champions and yell: "I AM BEAUTIFUL, I AM STRONG, I AM SMART. I AM A CHILD OF THE LIVING GOD. AND TODAY IS GOING TO BE AWESOME!"

I had those words printed on large canvases that hang in their bedrooms so they are the first words they see in the morning and the last they see at night. I am giving them a story, and I am praying they believe it. So that when the world comes at them and tells them that they are ugly, and dumb, and weak, they're just going to laugh in sheer confidence knowing it's a lie. In fact, it's so much of a lie that it even sounds stupid.

Step I is simple:

"Want something."

Step II is simple:

"Believe you *can* achieve what you want."

Post Chapter Questionnaire:

1. When you are alone, what are the words that you find yourself believing about yourself? These can be words you've given to yourself, or words that were given to you by someone else. Write these down.

2. Take yourself out of this now, and look at the list in front of you. If these words were *actually* true about someone (your neighbor, your child's school teacher, your sister in law, your own son, etc.), how successful do you think they could be? Are these words empowering, encouraging, successful, exciting, etc? Or are they insecure, defeating, disheartening, etc.?

   Your answer to question 2 is pivotal in determining whether you need new words. If this list of words sounds empowering, and uplifting, then rock out, but if these words sound horrible when applied to someone else, they're horrible when applied to you. We'll explore in later chapters why you deserve better words, but for now, I simply want you to replace them with words that speak life, give hope, and encourage the pursuit of your awesomeness. I understand this may seem fake, undeserved, un-real, or weird, but humor me.

3. If you need to, based on your answer to question 2, write a list of new words or phrases using the examples from the chapter, or ones that seem more authentic to you. Better yet, ask someone who knows you and loves you to write some for you. Often it's easier to believe them at first if they come from someone else.

Chapter III:

#JustANurse

"Your belief determines your action, and your action determines your results. But first, you have to believe." -Mark Victor Hansen, American inspirational author, creator of the Chicken Soup for the Soul *series.*

"Your circumstances do not define you. Expect a grand finale."- John Paul Warren, American author, speaker, difference maker

Earlier this year my wife and I visited friends out in Colorado Springs. One morning, over coffee, we were discussing what we might do that day when our friend, Lauren, jumped out of her seat. She ran to the counter, and excitedly returned with a pamphlet.

"OH MY GOODNESS! You guys have to go to Cave of the Winds and ride the Terror-Dactyl!"

She began showing us pictures of a beautiful gorge, amazing mountain views, and a visitor center with touristy gifts we could take home to the kids. At the top of the pamphlet printed in bold was some very exciting promotional text for this ride that had been "VOTED AMERICA'S #1 THRILL RIDE!".

"Okay, when you get there," she added, "don't even look around! Just go immediately to the desk and tell them you're going to ride the Terror-Dactyl. In fact, I totally *dare* you to go on it."

"Lauren, have you ever ridden this ride?"

"OH, ABSOLUTELY NOT! I would vomit before I even made it through the visitor's center, but you guys? You have to do it!"

Truth be told, I'm terrified of heights. However, I make a living coaching people on how to face and overcome their fear by seeing how irrational most fear actually is. Given this reality, I decided to take her dare, and use some of my own coaching advice. The drive there was beautiful! Coming from the Northeast (which is beautiful in its own right) the topography of Colorado is so foreign and breathtaking! We drove for about half an hour up into the mountains until we came to "Cave of the Winds".

Taking her advice, we parked, and were determined to walk right up to that ride and go before there was any chance to talk ourselves out of it. As we were walking into the visitor center, we passed a high ropes course built out over the gorge, and some cool hipster staff guys were running around on it.

"Hey guys! Welcome to Cave of the Winds! What we can we do for you?"

The voice was coming from way up in the sky. I had to squint through the sunlight to see the guy up at the top of the course.

"Oh, we're uh…we're here to ride the Terror-Dactyl."

"RIGHT ON! We haven't done our maintenance check on it yet though, so it'll be a little bit. If you just head on in to the visitor center, we'll have someone out there in a jiffy."

Taken aback, I thought, "WAIT! Did he say 'we haven't done our maintenance check?' OK. Still not gonna talk myself out of this. I had determined I would do it, and I will." We entered the visitor center, which has just about everything you'd want to see, except the Terror-Dactyl (at this point, I'm still not sure what this thing even is). My wife gets locked in on some cutesy trinkets for the kids. You know the ones that they'll inevitably break or lose within three days of us wasting our money on more crap they don't need. I started wandering aimlessly, trying to not think about this terrible mystery ride that is likely going to kill me.

I stepped outside to get some air. The balcony hung out over the gorge so far that I had to hold tight to the railing even though my feet were planted solidly on concrete. I breathe. Then a little deeper, as a last-ditch desperate attempt to calm my nerves. I went back inside. "What's taking them so long? Is the check going poorly?" I looked out the window to see a guy tethered to a cable spanning the gorge. He was only supported as high as his ankles while he stood upright like a tightrope walker. This is the maintenance check.

Far below him, there was a two-seater chair tied to the same cable. Apparently, participants were supposed to walk this plank, get into this chair, watch the floor underneath them disappear, and then free fall into the gorge before the cable catches and you ultimately find yourself swinging helplessly between two giant mountains.

To make matters worse, there were no videos of prior attempts for me to see an example (or proof that people actually survived). We were the only ones in line, so it wasn't like I could watch other people do it first. I didn't even have data or WiFi service on my phone to try and see if YouTube could offer me any insight into my fate. I just had to trust them. I didn't know them. I didn't know this ride. Even Lauren, who made me come here, had never done this ride. My stomach was upside down. There was literally no way I was going to do this.

I turned to Sonya, who had no emotional concern for the ride either way, and reminded her that for the same $100, we could totally have a nice brunch at an outdoor cafe with a couple mimosas! In her world mimosas beat almost anything, so I knew she'd be on board.

We drove away before they even finished the maintenance check.

What we believe inspires our action (and our inaction). As a result, you can tell exactly what someone believes based on what they do or don't do. For example:

- Some people believe in the physics of aviation so much that they're willing to straight up jump out of airplanes. Other people don't at all believe planes are at all safe, and they choose ground-based transportation altogether..

- Most people don't think twice about the safety of elevators and walk right on in, push their button, and then stand awkwardly silent (because nothing is scarier than being the first to talk on an elevator). Others, in turn, choose not to trust a small windowless box that could plummet stories with virtually no notice and they, instead, take the stairs (Sure, it's exercise, not fear — go with that!).

- Some people don't trust big agriculture so much that they decide to eat locally grown organic produce, and free-range, grass-fed animals, while others are rocking off-brand mac 'n' cheese with hot dogs and Pop Tarts.

- Some people believe in serial monogamy and the institution of marriage so strongly that they're willing to try it out three or four times! Others are still dating 15 years and 3 kids later.

This is a nod to the old axiom: "Actions speak louder than words." Our belief inspires our action to the degree that everything we do in our lives is simply because we believed two things about it:

1. It was worth doing.

2. We could do it.

If we hesitate on something, it's because we're hung up on one or both of these points. Maybe we think, "This is totally worth doing. In fact, it looks amazing, but I could never do it. It's great for other people, but it wouldn't be great for me." And so we don't do it. Maybe we think: "I'm awesome, and it's not that I'm being conceited, it's just that I've proven to be good at everything I've ever chosen to do, but *that*? That isn't worth my time. I would be good at it if I chose to do it, but the payout doesn't look worth the effort." And so we don't do it.

If you lead a team, a department, an entire business, or a family — you've seen this play out right before your eyes whether you were aware of it or not. Leaders are often incentivized to reward high performers. The leaders who aren't insecure actually enjoy rewarding high performers. But I've met very few leaders who are actually good at raising up high performers, which in my opinion, is the ultimate goal of a good leader.

See, when leaders set high performance goals, the only people who even aim to hit the goals are the people who have a rock solid foundational belief in themselves to be able to do it. For people to achieve or even attempt anything, they have to believe that it is both worth doing, and that they can do it. By rewarding high performers, leaders are influencing the single half of the equation that communicates: "Hitting this high performance goal is worth doing", however it doesn't touch the other half of the equation that asks, "but can I actually do it?"

Without influencing that half of the equation, leaders are calling out high performers to identify themselves, but aren't raising up potential high performers who have amazing ability but just lack confidence.

Think of your last office party. There was cake, a few people snuck in some flasks of whiskey in their coat pockets, someone hung a disco ball, and a random limbo line broke out. They started the limbo stick up at shoulder height and the whole office got in line for the fun. Sure, as it got lower, people were knocked out of the running for the glorious title of 'winner of the random office limbo competition", but some people impressed themselves with how well they did.

Now, imagine if the limbo stick had started at waist height. How many people would throw their hat in the ring and even attempt? Those same people who had fun, who felt some success, who impressed themselves, and got a boost of self-confidence wouldn't even be in line to try because the goal seemed out of reach. They might believe hitting the goal was worth it, but their disbelief in their ability caused them to not even try.

How many of us as parents incentivize our children to get "A"s on their report cards? We can raise the incentive to absurd heights, but until our children believe they can actually get As, all we're doing is telling them it's worth it — without helping them believe in their ability.

If you want to be a good leader, don't just call out and reward high performers, raise up new high performers. The way you're going to do that is by influencing both sides of the equation. You're going to continue to reward high performers because people need to believe that performing at a high level is actually worth it, but you're also going to help the other members of your team build their belief to the point they think that hitting that mark is even possible for them!

Let's arbitrarily call your high performance goal "Level X". Use that as a variable to apply to whatever you're leading. If you coach a baseball team, maybe it's 10 stolen bases or home-runs. If you're a parent, maybe it's a straight

"A" report card. If you lead a sales division, maybe it's $100,000 in monthly volume, or 100 units sold. Whatever the goal is, we're calling it "Level X".

Of course you want to reward the people who hit Level X! Hitting Level X is awesome. Maintaining it month over month is even better! But you have some amazing people on your team, who feel like Level X is so far away and so hard to hit, it just isn't worth trying. And increasing the reward for Level X doesn't inspire those people, it just makes them more acutely aware of what they're missing out on.

You need to lower the bar. Set a smaller goal for new people, or people who haven't come close to Level X. Don't set a goal based on their potential or ideal, set a goal based on their reality. Look at their last performance and their best ever performance, and maybe just challenge them to increase it by 10%. Maybe have your child focus on a single class and earn an "A" in that class. Maybe reward the girls who steal a single base for the first time.

What you're doing is setting the limbo bar at shoulder height and encouraging participation! People are going to step up. They're going to have fun. Some of them are going to impress themselves and you! And then you raise the goal and watch them hit it. Then you raise it again, and watch them hit it. Each time they hit the goal, they're building belief in themselves to be able to hit goals.

Once you become good at helping people believe in themselves, there is no limit to where your team, department, company, and family can go! If people are going to do something, they have to believe that it's both worth doing, and that they can actually do it.

For myself, my fear of the Terror-Dactyl was a bit of both. Was the thrill really worth the fear? Was the maintenance check really going to prove this thing was safe? Was I going to die? Was I bigger than other people who had previously been successful? Was I an outlier? I didn't need to see a therapist to understand that by driving away, my inaction betrayed the belief that I either didn't think it was worth it, or I didn't think I'd be successful at it.

Maybe it's the big purchase you financed that was totally worth it, with payments you knew (at least at the time) you could make. Maybe it was the committee you agreed to join that gave you influence over decisions, and doesn't require much time. It could be the puppy you chose not to buy because it wasn't worth the poop and pee all over the house at a time in life you're stressed without adding additional responsibilities. What about the medical career you didn't pursue? Even though you had the money, you weren't sure you were smart enough or driven enough to accomplish years of schooling.

Everything we do in life, is simply because we believe that it is both worth doing, and that we can do it. Helpful

73

ıt to remember when you want something from your ouse or children. If you can help them believe that it is worth their time and effort and that they'd be successful, they'll do it all on their own!

But this little truth is only descriptive, not prescriptive. That means it only describes why we make the decisions we make, it doesn't help us determine if those decisions are the best ones for us. Maybe that thing totally is worth doing, and our assessment was way off because it was based in fear. Maybe that awesome thing you really want isn't out of your reach at all, but your negative self-talk has made you doubt your natural abilities.

While our beliefs always determine our actions — again, to the degree that your actions show your true beliefs — it's the careful dance of words and thoughts that determine what we believe. This is why the last chapter was so important: The words you choose influence your thoughts, which influence your beliefs, which drive your actions.

If you're going to have different results in your life, you're going to have to take different actions. This is not rocket science. But it doesn't happen just because you want it to, or you have strong feelings about it, or you woke up sweating from a magical dream. You're actually going to have to build a new belief system, because as much as you might want to, you'll never act contrary to what you believe.

Building new beliefs only happens by having new thoughts, and you can only create those with new words.

But saying the words isn't enough. We have to truly believe them. Often, especially when we're new at this, the old negative beliefs are so ingrained and their roots are so deep, that as fast as we're taking on new words, the negative ones are swallowing them up. It's as if we're bailing water out of the boat, without realizing there's a hole in the bottom causing the water to be there in the first place.

Here's a subtle example of negative talk that permeates our language and sullies even the best of new words: "JUST". As in, "I'm just a nurse," or "I'm just a mom," or "I'm just a mechanic." The word "just", implies that there is a more noble position that you would be more proud to identify with. It implies that there's something else you want to be, or feel you should be, and that you settled. It implies that your current position, or identity, or person isn't as great as even you expect that it ought to be.

When you hear yourself say "just," understand that you're essentially saying, "I should be ____ ___, but I'm only ____ ." You're showing that deep down you believe that you missed the mark. That you failed or fell short. You show, even if it's just in subtle tones, that you believe you're a disappointment.

Get rid of "just." Look in the mirror and say it proudly: I'm a NURSE! I worked hard to get here! I care for people. I help people. My work is noble. I could have been a doctor, but I chose this path because it was better for me. I'm not here on accident. I didn't fail by achieving this. I chose this. It fits me. I'm a NURSE!"

Next time someone asks you what you do, don't say, "I'm *just* a mom". Practice saying this: "I work full-time to ensure that my next generation of world-changers has everything they need to be prepared for the giant task they're going to face when their time comes to effect powerful change. I could have been anything else, but I chose this. It's the most meaningful job in the world, and there's no where else I'd rather be!"

I watch my wife bear the unfair burden of mom-guilt constantly. She'll tell herself, "I *should* play more with the kids." "I *shouldn't* let them watch so much TV." "I *should…*" Should. Want to. Wish.

It's not just moms who allow their mental framework to invite guilt. We are constantly using words that invite shame and guilt. Instead of "should", try saying "choose" or "will". Should invites shame, while choose and will are empowering.

We can say powerful new daily affirmative phrases every 15 minutes on a timer, but if deep down we believe we're "less than," "unworthy," "disappointments," then we're just whitewashing a broken fence. And a broken fence, no matter how shiny it is, can't do its job effectively.

Nursing was a second profession for me. When I went back to school I was one of only a handful of guys in a predominantly female class, which is pretty typical in the nursing world. Most of my classmates were just out of high school pursuing their first degree, and I remember the first day we were orienting on a medical-surgical unit in a hospital. We had oriented at other hospitals and on other units before, but never here. It was new. Like anything new, a lot of us were nervous. We didn't know who was who. We didn't know where to stand, or who to talk to, or where to put our stuff. We wanted to be helpful, but we didn't want to get in the way, and we didn't know how to navigate that line.

I was pretty comfortable in my own skin by this point, which made for a fun time watching my classmates writhe inside with their nerves almost palpable. On this first morning, we were standing in a big group in the hallway kind of waiting for further instruction. One of the staff nurses was pushing a patient toward us in a wheelchair and yelled out, "Coming through, c'mon guys, move to the sides." Another nurse was pushing her med-cart down the hallway and asked, "Can you guys move to one side or the other so we can get through?"

In my mind, these were perfectly fine interactions. We were a large group taking up a small hallway. The staff nurses legitimately had a job to do. I didn't think they were mean, or gruff, I thought they were matter-of-fact, just doing their jobs. As the group of us eventually made it to the break room to put our stuff down, I heard several of the girls from my class talking:

"Uggghhh, the nurses on this unit are bitches…"

"I'd never want to work here, nobody is nice. Nobody came over and said hi to us, or smiled at us, or welcomed us or anything."

"Ew…this is gonna be the longest semester ever if we have to keep coming back here."

I was quick to point out that while we were standing in the hallway, none of us smiled, said hi, or introduced ourselves to any of the staff nurses. I could guarantee that some of those nurses were talking to each other at the water cooler:

"Ugggghhh, the students from this class are bitches…"

"I'd never want one of them to work with us. Nobody is nice. Nobody came over and said hi to us, or smiled at us, or introduced themselves or anything."

"Ew…this is gonna be the longest semester ever if we have to keep seeing them."

People often reflect back what they're given. If you smile, they'll smile back. If you say hi and ask how they are, they'll say hi and ask how you are. If you walk confidently, with your head up and your shoulders back, people will read you as confident and competent. If you give a firm handshake and make eye contact, people will believe in you. The opposite is also true.

All too often we make assumptions about how people see us. As a result, we feel judged, unworthy, or exposed. We feel like people don't like us, or don't trust us, or wouldn't buy from us, or partner with us, when the truth of it is there's a strong possibility that they are just reflecting back what they're given. How you assume people read you has nothing to do with how they actually read you, and everything to do with how you perceive yourself! If you feel unworthy of success, that will show, and people will reflect that back to you.

Maybe you were abused verbally or sexually by someone who was supposed to protect you causing you to live with deep shame, distrust and insecurity. Maybe you inherited a victim-hood mindset from generations of forefathers who were beaten and chained and forced to believe that their freedom didn't exist, and because you carry that, you find yourself blaming others for your failures. Maybe you were given a silver spoon and every possible advantage, but you squandered it, leaving you with such self-doubt that it runs deep into your core. Maybe you were raised with sugar and spice and everything nice, and you never had to work for anything, so you're stuck wondering why life isn't giving you what you feel entitled to.

It's not enough to believe you can be successful if you deeply believe that you are unworthy of success. As long as you don't believe that you are worthy of achieving your wildest dreams, then you'll find a way to negate any progress toward it that you do achieve.

For example:

- You want an intimate, honest relationship with a great guy, but every time you're with someone who might actually be good for you, you freak out, get weird, and sabotage it.

- You want to open that flower shop, and every time that loan application letter comes in the mail, you freeze, imagine yourself failing, and throw it away before you even fill it out.

- You want to earn partner at the firm, but every time you're in a position to talk about your achievements and chat about the value you add, you remember past words of worthlessness, and you instead launch into self-deprecating humor, minimizing yourself and your role.

- You want to get the exclusive listing for that prestige million-dollar home, but you have a lot of competition and can't think of a single reason why they'd choose you. Your insecurity causes you to stop following up because you can't make a confident argument to promote yourself.

I met Mike during our freshman year of college. In a small, private school, Mike stuck out like a sore thumb. He had bold, colorful tattoos. He used bold, colorful language. He wore the same ripped green cargo shorts almost everyday with the ragged seams stuck together with nothing but silver duct tape.

In a place that valued conformity, Mike refused to conform. He challenged the status quo, he rebelled against the "should" and the "ought to", and found himself without many friends, except for me. His boldness to look, talk, and act differently repelled people and made others uncomfortable, but it attracted me. We went on to be best men in each others' weddings, and we call ourselves best friends to this day.

Mike was fascinating to me in college, because while he was one of the smartest people I've ever met, he sucked at school. He couldn't make friends. His professors rolled their eyes at his perceived immaturity, and he began to reflect back the disdain he perceived, which only made things worse. Within two years Mike had failed out of school (though he'll joke that it was a "mutual parting of ways"), found a job waiting tables at a local diner, and slept on a friend's beat up apartment sofa that had been previously rescued from a dumpster.

To meet Mike now in his huge brick home, decorated by his beautiful wife like a Pinterest board, and tucked away securely at the end of a cul-de-sac in an upscale suburb south of Nashville, you'd never guess his story. You'd never guess that his parents cycled between drug abuse and rehab, or that his mom couldn't hold down a job while his dad could barely pay the bills. You'd never guess that the only attention he received as a child were sporadic reminders of his worthlessness in the midst of long periods of simply being ignored.

Mike grew up believing you go on strike to get ahead and resort to substances to numb the pain of a sucky reality. He was shown that when the substances got too hard to control, you were supposed to run to rehab and start all over again with no real hope of ever ending the cycle. He was taught to mask insecurity with bravado and machismo. Yelling, fighting, and hitting even the people you love were acceptable. He grew up believing he was worthless, that he was a drain on the family. He believed that he was unworthy of anything good — he had never seen what good even looked like.

When I met Mike in college he was broken inside with a tough exterior shell. Though he was easily one of the smartest people I had ever met, he couldn't focus that energy on a productive scholastic assignment because (in his mind) if he got a good grade from the teacher it might look like he cared. He couldn't get himself to dress, act, talk, or perform academically like everyone else because he didn't believe he was worthy of love, acceptance, success, or even kudos.

Soon after failing out of school, and reeling from the expected scorn dished out by his father, Mike sought professional help from a licensed therapist. In just a handful of sessions, he was able to reframe his story. He realized that he was a survivor of his upbringing and not a victim! He realized that his ceiling wasn't limited or defined by his past, or his parents, and that there was an undetermined future that he could write. Mike decided to try. He decided to care.

He climbed off of the recycled couch, enrolled in a program at Rutgers University, and from there earned a seat at John Marshall Law School in Chicago. He became the president of his graduating law class, honed his craft, and now earns a multiple six-figure salary serving as the president of a premier sports training corporation with locations all across the country.

Mike still has colorful tattoos, and still uses colorful language. And while his pants are no longer duct-taped together, you'll almost never see him in a collared shirt or tie. Most importantly, he is still fiercely independent, but not out of macho defiance and insecurity. He walks boldly because he has become so confident in his ability to produce excellence that he is no longer insecure. His wife is on a pedestal and adored, and their young daughter is shown daily in words and actions that she is beautiful, and strong, and smart.

There are people and circumstances in your past who cause you to believe that you are defined by them. They whisper lies to your heart that you can't rise above what you've done or what's been done to you. They convince you that your ceiling is limited, that you are broken, injured, or damaged goods. You may find yourself believing that you are unworthy of love, unworthy of success, or that you will never amount to anything. If you are going to achieve your heart's true dream of wild success, then you have to shed the victimhood mindset. You have to, like Mike, realize that you are an overcomer, powerful to effect change, and worth more than you could ever imagine!

 Some of your friends may sometimes have good advice, or sometimes offer a good listening ear, but other times their advice sucks and should not be taken under any circumstances.

That can be accomplished in a couple ways, and those ways aren't mutually exclusive of each other. Like Mike, you may need to see a professional who is an expert at helping people reframe their stories. Some of your friends may sometimes have good advice, or sometimes offer a good listening ear, but other times their advice sucks and should not be taken under any circumstances. It's not that they don't mean well, it's just that they have no idea what they're doing. You didn't let Uncle Larry bring his boombox and his mix-tape to DJ your wedding because that day deserved a professional. Doesn't your life deserve that same respect?

I was speaking with my sister recently, and she explained how God speaks to her in imagery. One image He gave her was of herself at 8 years old in the basement, bound by heavy chains like a boa constrictor.

She looks at God with her innocent eyes, and says, "Why am I in chains?"

He looks back and says, "Dear daughter, look: those chains aren't attached to anything. I've already done the work of breaking them, you just have to put them down."

Looking for clarity, she replies, "then why do I feel so afraid?"

"Because the chains you're holding are chains of fear. You're wrapped in fear. Put them down."

"But God, I don't know if I can."

"Look at your arms, and your legs. Look at the size of your muscles and realize your power. You got those muscles from holding those chains for so long. Why don't you now choose to put them down and use your strength for something awesome!"

Often we learn to identify with the chains so intimately that we no longer know who we are without them. Many of us have been carrying chains of shame, and fear, and insecurity for so many years that we have come to believe that they're simply part of who we are. They're not. They can be broken. Sometimes they already are. You just have to put them down.

Secondly, millions across the world have found hope, value and worth in the person of Jesus. I'm not saying that a lot of those same people aren't bigoted, small minded, and judgmental (which is a shame because Jesus Himself was none of those things). In the person of Jesus we find someone in whom no failure is bigger than His love or His forgiveness or His sacrifice. We find someone who loves everybody, whose life was worth giving for everybody! We find someone who says "No matter who you are, what you've done, or where you've been, you are loved, accepted, and worthy!"

If your experience with the church or with people who claim to follow Jesus has been one of judgement, hatred, or bigotry, you've not met Jesus. You've met people. And people can sometimes suck! I'm not here to preach, and if this doesn't speak to you, then ignore it, but sometimes stuff gets broken so badly, only its Creator can really fix it and redeem it for greatness.

Step I is simple:

"Want something."

Step II is simple:

"Believe you can achieve what you want."

Step III is simple:

"Believe you are worthy of achieving what

you want."

Post Chapter Questionnaire:

1. Have you really wanted to do something that you've been resisting? Are you resisting it because you're not sure it's worth doing, or because you're not sure you'd be good at it? It's important to recognize if the hesitation is coming because you don't believe in the thing, or if you don't believe in yourself.

2. Do you secretly (or not secretly) assume that people look down on you or think poorly of you because of your current position in life? Often the way we see ourselves is how we assume other people see us. So if we find ourselves assuming that people see us as chubby, under-achieving, unworthy — it usually has nothing to do with them; it is instead a window to how we view ourselves.

3. Do you carry shame from your past that you assume people will judge you for?

4. Do you look down on you, or think poorly of yourself because of your current position in life, or the shame from your past?

5. Do you frequently use self-deprecating humor or belittling language when talking about yourself?

6. How do you think your attitude would change if you were to value yourself, forgive yourself, only speak highly of yourself, and believe that others respect and admire you?

7. Here's an exercise. Try writing this, or something similar, and then reading it out loud:

"I am not defined or limited by my circumstances, or my past mistakes. I am more powerful than what happens to me, and even if I can't change it, I can choose my reaction to it. I am fierce. I have no ceiling. I deserve amazing things, and I am strong enough to go get them. Neither my past, nor my present circumstances are strong enough to stop me."

Chapter IV:

#StatisticallyAverage

"Faith is all about believing. You don't know how it will happen, but you know it will." Author is unknown, but this quote was retweeted by Steph Curry, so it's legit.

"The reasonable person adapts their self to the world, the unreasonable one persists in trying to adapt the world to their self. Therefore, all progress depends on the unreasonable person." -George Bernard Shaw, Irish playwright whose legacy far outlived his critics.

"There has to be something more"

It was the summer of 2001 and Jeremy had just finished his first year of teaching business education at a high school in Virginia. He was sitting in his kitchen staring blankly at a stale income chart: "I have to work for 30 years to cap out at $70,000 per year." He was a fresh-faced graduate of James Madison University and while he didn't hate teaching, it proved to be different than what he thought he had signed up for.

The initial appeal of time freedom — those illustrious evenings and summers off — proved to be a mirage. With an annual salary of only $28,600, he found himself giving away his evenings selling tickets to sporting events and spending summers selling watercraft at the local marina. As the son of a coal miner and a stay at home mom- he learned to love the outdoors. He specifically loved duck hunting, but the season was only open for two months, and Sunday hunting was prohibited. That left only eight days in a whole year that he could enjoy what he most loved in this world.

"There has to be something more to life, and until I own my time, I'll never be able to experience it."

As a humble teacher, that haunting thought of wanting something more was the spark that led Jeremy, in just 15 years, to build 8 different companies, all focused on passive income, which positions him as one of the wealthiest people within his Washington, D.C. suburb. But to speak to him, you'll quickly realize that he never cared about money as an end itself. He wanted to be a teacher because he thought he could own his time. Once that proved to be untrue, he set out to build wealth that would pay him without requiring his time. The way he says it, "Jim, I'll always throw renewable resource at non-renewable. I can always make more money. I can never make more time." He now has the freedom to work when, where, and how he wants. He can explore life with his family by plane, by sea, or by land. He can enjoy the best restaurants, museums, vacations, and leisure activities. As I write this, he and his family are preparing to go to Colorado for 7 months just because they can.

He's visited Colorado and when he's there he rubs shoulders with wealthy businessmen who fly in and out weekly on their private jets. They're curious how Jeremy can live their lifestyle without seemingly having to do anything compared to the demands they have. "It's simple," Jeremy says, "They may have more money than me, but my aim was never to make money, my aim was to own my time so I could live a lifestyle I loved. I knew that in order to do that, I'd have to develop passive income, so every company I created and built was with that goal in mind."

We talked in the previous two chapters about how if you're going to be successful, it's not enough to know what you want, you have to actually believe you can achieve it and believe you're worthy of it! Therein lies the rub for a lot of people. If you're going to be successful, you're going to have to actually believe that it's inevitable. And not just "kind of" believe, where you hope, and pray, and wish, and want in the secret of your heart while you're lying in your bed with the lights out. You have to believe like you're standing on the cliff of a mountain shouting your success to the whole world like you've already achieved it, and now you're just walking toward its inevitability. You have to believe in your success so much that you could confidently put on a suit, stand in front of people who intimidate you, and tell them exactly where you're going as if there isn't a question or a hesitation in the world. Because for successful people, there isn't.

Jeremy learned in his summers at the marina that he was actually pretty good at sales, and when a co-worker mentioned a real estate opportunity, he thought very simply: "Well, if I can sell boats during a drought, I can probably sell houses." He started attending evening classes, and studying on the weekends. When the school year ended in 2003, he didn't tell his principal that it was his last, but he was going to give real estate everything he had that summer. He hasn't gone back to teaching.

In 2004, after proving to be a very good realtor, he got married and bought the brokerage firm that he had worked for. Life was looking up, his trajectory seemed unstoppable... and then Hurricane Katrina hit and the economy shut down. "Ask a lot of people, Jim, and they'll talk about the recession in 2007/2008, but realtors know the phone stopped ringing as soon as the hurricane hit.

"In 2006, I couldn't sell a house. I had a team. I had full-time employees. By 2007 I was living purely off of equity. Our trajectory was only negative. There was literally no income. My buyers' agents were leaving the brokerage. I couldn't beg anyone to sell their house, because they owed more than it was worth. I didn't know where or how it was going to end, but I knew I'd find a way."

Do you want to know why believing in inevitable success is so hard for most people? It's hard because there is often no evidence, or logic, or reason in the world to make that decision. For the conservative gamblers among us, it's often hard or impossible to place that bet. And if we do place that bet, it's a half hearted one, and we've hedged it a little with a bet to the opposite just to mitigate our losses. I hear it all the time:

"Jim, I've tried 172 diets in the last 10 years, and I haven't stuck to one. Why would I believe in my success now?"

"Jim, there are 413 resumes on that desk, and mine won't stand out in any way. Why would they hire me?"

"Jim, I'm shy and I don't know how to promote myself. I want my business to succeed, but I can't help but feel like it isn't in the cards for me."

"Jim, my wife and I can't even speak to each other without stepping on emotional landmines, and I don't see a way out. I want our marriage to succeed, but I just don't know how it's going to."

I asked Jeremy how he knew to press on when people were bailing left and right.

"Maybe the best answer to this question is a history lesson. After coming ashore with his army, the 16th-century Spanish conquistador, Cortes, ordered to have all of their ships burned. This sent a message to his army that they would either win the battle or die trying, there was no turning back and retreat was not an option.

"When you study individuals who have accomplished great levels of success, many share a common thread. They gave themselves no escape route. All too often we set goals and plan for success while still holding on to a safety net. This safety net should be called a "hinder net," as all it does is hinder you from reaching your dreams. When you allow for an escape route or a safety net, the first time you experience adversity you will be reminded that you don't have to keep pushing forward. Trust me, when you set out to do and accomplish big things, YOU WILL BE HIT WITH ADVERSITY! When adversity hits and you have nowhere to go but through it, you find a way to succeed where you never thought it was possible.

"I was in the middle of likely the worst real estate crash in history. I had a choice to make. I could either limp along and sell real estate and make ends meet until something stabilized in the market, or I could go for my dream. Going for my dream got my vote! In order to do so I 'burned the ships!'" I remember spending nearly all of my savings on the education that I needed to make the proper decisions. I stopped *just* selling real estate and made success my only option. When adversity hit I had no choice but to push on and figure out a way to succeed."

Jeremy became incredibly wealthy through real estate in one of the worst market crashes in history. He had no business doing that. Nobody would have placed a bet on him, because it wouldn't have made any sense! There were firms with far more experience and capital than he had. Statistically, an outfit of his size, in an established market, with no capital, a negative financial trajectory, a disheartened staff, and little experience should have been the first to fold. Instead, he so far outshined he peers, that very little property, either residential or commercial, exchanges hands in Fredericksburg, Virginia and its surrounding region today without one of Jeremy's companies playing a role.

My first stint in undergrad was at a small Bible college just outside of Philadelphia. I finished with my bachelor's, but switched my major three times and left there having no idea what I wanted to do with my life. And if leaving college with a bunch of loans, no job, no vision, nowhere to live, and no direction wasn't enough of a bummer, I was left with deep existential wounds and questions I couldn't resolve.

I thought something must be wrong with me. They taught God like a fact of life that I should have already known. He exists. He picked some guys to write the Bible for Him, and they did a perfect job. Get on board, or get left behind. And it seemed like everyone got on board. Except me. I learned to do and to say the right things to fit in, but in my heart and my soul, there was a storm brewing. How can I believe in a God that I didn't see? What evidence was there? The world seems pretty random. A lot of shit happens to even good people. So even if there was a God, what was the benefit in serving Him?

I confided in some close friends that these questions were haunting me. They pointed me in the direction of some books written by really smart people who explained away questions with deep psychological talk. But it all seemed like rationalizing the problem after the fact, and remained totally unsatisfactory to me. They weren't answers. They were explanations that only worked for people who already believed.

It wasn't until years later that I realized a very important truth: I cannot defend with any logic at all whether God exists, and neither can anyone else! Belief requires faith, and sometimes faith is just a matter of making a choice and sticking with it. While I couldn't win an argument with an atheist about the existence of God, I chose to believe in God anyway. I made the conscious choice to believe that myself and everyone around me were created by a God who genuinely loves us, created us on purpose, and for a purpose. And He wants us to kick ass!

What's funny, ironic, and powerful is what happened after I made that choice. I started to experience hope, love, and joy in a way that I never knew before. I started to experience peace beyond understanding even in the middle of crisis situations. I started to see miracles where I used to see coincidence. I started to want the best for others in a way that stirred my heart to give and to serve. It was almost like my choice to believe in God made God real to me. It made me aware of Him. It plugged me into a higher power that was always available to me, but I had no way to access it before.

I still can't tell you with any logical or rational certainty why I believe God exists. But I can tell you the power of making that seemingly unreasonable choice, and walking forward as if it were powerfully true, has changed my life. That life change affirmed my decision, which has made me walk more confidently toward a belief in God. Walking even more confidently then opened up more awareness of love, joy, and peace, which affirmed my decision even further and emboldened me to walk with even more certainty, until this positive feedback loop has driven doubt so far from my mind it doesn't even exist as an option any longer. Of course God exists! It seems like foolishness to think otherwise.

This is why people of faith can seem crazy! They live and act with an assurance that has no rational or logical foundation, except for their personal experience of profound life change. Their decision was made in faith. My decision was made in faith. But the life change that happened as a result of that decision was very real and tangible and confirmed with absolute certainty to me that God is real!

This choice to believe was unnerving for some of my friends. They thought I lost my mind. They thought I drank some Kool-Aid. They started 'round-the-clock' watches to make sure my insanity wasn't going to hurt people. They questioned me. They doubted me. To them I had clearly lost reason. There was no evidence. The existence of God was impossible based on anything they could see, and, at the very least, so improbable it wasn't worth pursuing.

> Your success depends on the choice to believe in something that you can't yet see, and to walk toward it as if it's truth is absolute.

Your success depends on the choice to believe in something that you can't yet see, and to walk toward it as if it's truth is absolute. Here's why:

When you base your goals and your decisions and set your vision only on what is evident, logical, rational, reasonable, probable, or likely, you are never going to do anything extraordinary. By every statistical measure, Jeremy was supposed to fail. He knew nothing about real estate, had to deal with the worst crash in history, and had powerful competitors. He was supposed to give up and go back to teaching.

Anybody can make a decision based on evidence and likelihood. In fact, our natural fear of loss and aversion to failure prompt us to only make those choices that are likely to turn out in our favor. But when everybody is making those choices, it becomes ordinary and average. If you want to be extraordinary, if you want to achieve something amazing, you're going to have to believe that something you've never achieved and never done is absolutely going to happen.

There isn't going to be any evidence for this decision. In fact, there might be an entire lifetime of evidence telling you the opposite, but you're going to have to choose to believe in its inevitability anyway. You are going to have to slay a hundred giants and leap a thousand hurdles between you and your goal. It is going to be hard. And if you don't have to do it, you won't. It won't be worth it.

If you aren't certain that your story ends in a place of amazing fulfillment and success, then you're going to wonder at every hurdle if this is how far you get. Every giant you're going to look up at will make you question if it's worth it. You'll think: Maybe I've gone far enough. I've done pretty well. I can stop here, right? If stopping is an option, you'll take it. If you've set up a Plan B or a back-up plan, it's going to act as a Siren calling you to easier waters and

> If you aren't certain that your story ends in a place of amazing fulfillment and success, then you're going to wonder at every hurdle if this is how far you get.

greener pastures. Nothing is more important to your success than belief, and nothing betrays your lack of belief like a back-up plan.

"Have to" is a brilliant motivator. I remember a story that was told to me when I was young. It was a story of a general ordering troops to pull a very heavy cannon to the top of a hill. I don't know why they didn't use horses or trucks. Maybe they didn't have horses or trucks. Don't press me on details. It was probably a made-up story anyway.

So the general gives the order, "Hey guys, you need to pull that cannon to the top of the hill."

And the guys are like, "Umm, General, there are only like 100 of us, and the cannon really is super heavy…"

And the general says, "I know all that. That's why there's a star on my shoulder. It's proof that I know stuff. So get that cannon up there."

And the guys respond: "But General, there's no way we can do that!"

So the general replies, "FINE! Then I'm going to be forced to kill half of you."

Obviously the troops are like, "Okay, okay, we'll give it our best go, but honestly, that threat was a little over reactive and harsh, no?" So they push and pull and struggle, but they can't get it up the hill.

Exhausted now, they say to the General, "Yeah, so, like we said, we can't get it up the hill."

And the general goes, "Yeah, so, like I said, I'm killing half of you." So he did. I don't know how. Maybe he called in air strike, or he had an elite force of snipers with rifles already aimed at the half he had planned to kill. Or again, this might just be totally made up. But when he was done, he looks at the remaining 50 guys and goes, "So, ummm…sorry about your friends and everything. No hard feelings, but you seriously have to go get that cannon up the hill."

Horrified now, the guys say, "Ummm…General, you can't just kill our friends and say 'no hard feelings.' There are definitely hard feelings. And I don't know if you noticed that we couldn't get it up the hill even *with* our friends, there's no way we're gonna do it without them."

And the general said, "Well, then I'm gonna have to kill half of you."

Those 50 guys push and pull and kick and scream, and sure enough, they can't move the cannon up the hill. And true to his word, the general kills half of them once again. He then goes to the remaining 25 guys and says,

"Ummm…so…I know things are a bit awkward between us right now, but I hope you at least realize how serious I am about getting that cannon up there. So yeah, you're gonna have to get that cannon up the hill."

Faced with absolute certainty about their fate should they fail, the 25 soldiers pulled and pushed that cannon up the hill when 100 of them couldn't. When robbed of a way out, they were only left with the option to succeed. Despite the unlikeliness of that story's ties to truth, the moral remains: It is amazing what we can accomplish when we don't have the luxury of failing! It is equally amazing how wimpy we will allow ourselves to be if we have a way out.

I learned this valuable lesson in my days as a runner. Thankfully the "Sweat Pants Master" era of sarcastic glory came to an end, and I reached a point early in college where I was ready to shed the "chubby" label also. I started running. At first it was just a half mile, because let's be honest, running is usually the punishment coaches dole out in most sports. I can still hear my high school football coach yelling: "LARSEN! WRONG COUNT. FOUR LAPS!" At that point in my life, if I wasn't running *from* something, I wasn't running. And in most circumstances, even in "fight or flight" mode, I usually assured myself that I'd fare better in "fight."

Eventually, however, I learned to love running. That half-mile soon became a mile, which became 3, then 5, then

10. Before long I was running half-marathons, and full marathons and having a jolly time all along the way. But I realized something in my training. If I decided to run 6 miles, and I found a 2-mile loop right outside my dorm room, it was very hard to run that loop three times. I'd run around it once, and the sight of the eventual finish line would tempt me to stop short of my goal.

I'd start thinking: "Two miles really is good enough for today. I mean, you did a long run yesterday, and you have some other stuff you could totally be doing instead. I think the guys are playing *GoldenEye* in the recreation room. Just call it a day, and do a longer one tomorrow."

In order to run the full 6, I'd have to shut that voice off, no matter how good video games sounded at that moment, and push myself to make the next loop. And, inevitably, as I came around to my dorm room, that voice would be yelling at me this time:

"Okay dude, seriously! Four miles is pretty close to 6. I mean, actually, if you stopped now, your body wouldn't even notice the difference! It's like the same thing. Plus, if you shower now you can get in the cafeteria line earlier for pizza night! Last week, they were completely out of buffalo chicken by the time you got there!"

Pizza night is a legit distraction! But the reality is, I brought the failure on myself by allowing an "out." I learned that if I was going to run 6 miles, I had to run straight out for 3 miles, so that I had no choice but to run 3 miles home. When we remove the back up plan, we have no choice, and "have to" is an amazing motivator.

Running may differ than business, but the rules for success are the same. My first taste of success in business came with a network marketing company. During that time, I got to know a lot of successful people as we became very successful ourselves. I started the work of distinguishing the traits of successful people from unsuccessful people. I can't even tell you how many of the success stories started with a desperate: "I *had* to make it work."

Your success starts with a decision. It's a simple choice to believe that success is actually inevitable. Jen Sincero is a hero of mine. She is also my constant travel companion, despite being completely unaware of my existence, and only traveling with me via audible.com. She says it this way: "So often, we pretend we've made a decision, when what we've really done is signed up to try until it gets too uncomfortable."

I heard of a study in conversation that said 93 percent of successful businesses had to abandon their original business plans because they were not working. The methods that ultimately made them successful were not those which they had initially planned to use. The point is that if you spend all your financial and emotional capital up front trying to launch your business, you'll have nothing left to make the necessary adjustments to the feedback you receive. This is absolutely true in life as well as business. There are no smooth rides. The better and more fully you understand that, the more prepared you'll be to tackle it.

On the road to success, you will meet failure! You will be defeated in some battles. You will get overwhelmed and you will get knocked down. You will get discouraged, and you will wonder if it's all worth it. If you spend all of your energy and capital on your original plan and it doesn't work, will you be able to rally for another round? When does it become too hard for you? When is the pursuit of success no longer worth it? When is the giant too big, or the obstacle too high?

Statistically speaking, Jeremy should have failed. Half of realtors fail in their first handful of years and only a small portion of the ones who remain are making more than a modest middle-class income. Teaching was a "sure thing." Why would he leave a guarantee to pursue such long odds?

The answer lies in a truth that only successful people understand: Humans are not statistics. Unless you're playing a true game of pure chance, where the playing field is completely equal, then the chances of your success are either 100 percent or 0 percent. You will either succeed or not and it has nothing to do with how well other people have done previously.

When you're making a decision like: "Should I take this risk and start this business?", or "Should I pursue medical school?", or "Should I get married?", etc. Do your research and understand statistically how well other people have done, but realize that those statistics don't determine your results! All those statistics tell you is the percentage of people that didn't give up!

Now, if a venture has a high percentage of failure that doesn't mean it isn't worth pursuing, or that you're likely to fail. It simply means that a lot of people have thrown in the towel and given up before succeeding. That should raise flags and prompt questions, but it doesn't mean you need to retreat.

Ask why people are giving up. There's a reason for it. Is the continuing overhead too demanding? Is there very little support? Is the sample size too small to actually draw any conclusions from? Does it require a level of motivation and drive that most people don't possess? You might learn that the reason people are quitting doesn't actually apply to you at all.

I watch people regularly shy away from amazing opportunities because statistically not many people succeed. You are not a statistic. You are not a chance. You have heart and ambition. And you have a mission. You have power, purpose, and passion! Don't underestimate yourself and your ability to overcome the obstacles that might derail others!

Thomas Edison, in his invention of the lightbulb is quoted as saying, "I didn't fail 1,000 times. The light bulb was an invention with 1,000 steps." Another way he's quoted is, "I didn't fail, I just found 1,000 ways it didn't work." If you're committed to your absolute and ultimate success, then failure simply becomes an absolute and necessary step in refining the plan. Your original plan won't work. Period. You're going to meet with failure, and you'll either use that lesson to make a better plan, or you're going to give up altogether. You will face a crossroad after failure where you're forced to choose whether you'll regroup with another plan or give up. And that cycle will only play out as many times as your grit and determination allow. You'll either let it play out as many times as it requires until you reach your goal, or you'll stop letting it play out because you've gotten far enough. You knock on the door to success until it either breaks down or you get tired of knocking.

If you're going to be successful, you have to make the choice that you will be successful. You have to choose that, come hell or high water, you will not lose. You have to do as Jeremy did and "burn the ships." You will have to overcome whatever stands in your way on your way to victory. But you'll only do that if what you want is bigger than the obstacle you're facing. You'll only win if you believe winning is possible. And you'll only succeed if you believe you're worthy of it. You have to want something. You have to believe you can do it and that you're worthy of it, and then you have to decide that you will do it.

Making that decision to believe in your inevitable success is scary! It defies reason! It doesn't make sense! We find it much easier to hope and wish for our dreams in the quiet of our hearts rather than to speak it into existence. If we put it out there, people might laugh at us, or think we're crazy, or even worse, they might hold us accountable and ask us how it's going (when we already know full well, we never really intended to actually do it!). When Jeremy told his in-laws that he wouldn't be returning to the classroom, their jaws dropped! Why would he trade a certain salary, with benefits and a retirement plan for something so uncertain!?!

To be successful, you have to choose to be successful. And then, you're going to have to tell people. Out loud.

Now, I know that for most people making a decision without any evidence in favor of it is excruciatingly hard and almost impossible. That's honestly why ordinary is common, and extraordinary is rare. But let's talk about 'normal' for a minute.

Normal is defined by the majority. It literally is what is typical or expected of the average or ordinary person. But here's the thing, also by definition, ordinary is not extraordinary.

We worry about how people will perceive us when we put ourselves and our dreams out there because they may judge us and think that we have no shot, or that our goal is unrealistic. We don't want to be unrealistic. We naturally want to conform to 'normal' to be part of the herd. But if we strive to conform to normal and ordinary, we will never achieve anything extraordinary. Are you following how powerful this is?

I love this definition of obsession: "A persistent, disturbing preoccupation with an often unreasonable idea…" Whew — that is just gold!

Ask any doctor if medical school required a bit of an obsession. Ask any athlete if elevating their game from hobby to profession required a bit of an obsession. As any entrepreneur if taking their business to the next level required a bit of an obsession. Ask Jeremy's wife Jessica, if building his business required a little bit of an obsession.

You can't be better than average without a season of a persistent disturbing preoccupation with an unreasonable idea. Success isn't reasonable. It's not realistic. It's not statistically likely. And if you strive to conform to what is reasonable, likely, realistic — then you will always remain average.

Like Jeremy, you are going to have to develop a preoccupation with the unreasonable idea that you might actually be freaking awesome and that your great idea might blow up! And that preoccupation will disturb people who don't get it. And you'll have to be okay with that, because your success depends on it.

I want to offer something that will help to make that decision easier for you:

You know the hypothetical glass that people debate whether it's half-full or half-empty? Your answer to that question is everything. The people who see the glass as half empty are pessimists. They hate being called that, so don't call them pessimists, because they'll get their undergarments all bunched up. They prefer the term "realist."

"Jim, I'm not a pessimist, I'm a *realist*. I'm just calling it like it is and not sugar-coating it."

No, you're a pessimist and no one wants to hang out with you. When you see the glass as half-empty, your focus is on what you don't have. You're seeing the empty part of the glass. When you're focused on what you don't have, you get jealous, envious, bitter, and you live a life that's utterly unsatisfying because you're failing to appreciate everything that you do have right in front of you.

I want you to imagine standing in your yard facing a privacy fence that stands between you and your neighbor's house. You can't see through the fence, but you can see above it. If the fence was only waist high, you could see right over it, and hand beer back and forth with your neighbor on nice summer evenings. If the fence were eight feet tall you'd never know what your neighbor was up to. We're going to call this privacy fence "EXPECTATION."

I want you to understand that 'expectation' is a fence that each of us builds at varying heights, and in varying places every day. We build this fence of expectation all the time. We stand facing it and we can only see something that is taller than the fence, or exceeds our "expectation." Anything less than the height of our expectation is lost to view on the other side of the fence.

For instance, you may frequent a particular restaurant that by every measure provides amazing service. The first time you went there, you were amazed! You had virtually no expectations so your fence was very low and you noticed and appreciated everything. The aroma was sweet, the staff was friendly, the presentation of the food was exquisite, etc. This amazing experience caused you to raise that fence of expectation up a bit. The next time you went there it was good, but not great. The decline in your reaction had nothing to do with the actual experience, but everything to do with your experience compared to the height of your fence. Now that you've been there a dozen times you barely notice any details. You've raised the fence up so high that the little things you used to appreciate so much can't even be seen any longer.

We raise these fences of expectation everywhere. We raise them on our spouses, until we can't see anything that they're doing on the other side. We look up above the top of the fence, but we can't see them up there because they're down below working on the other side. Our expectations of them are so high that all we notice is how they're not meeting or exceeding them. Right in front of our noses, we miss everything that they're actually doing for us every single day. And the ironic thing is that a lot of those things we fail to notice now are the very things we fell in love with them for before we raised up the fence.

We raise the fence on our kids and we expect so much of them. These expectations cause us to miss everything they're doing because we're only focused on what they're not doing. We see what they're not achieving. We see who they're not becoming. We see what hobbies they've not taken up. And if we would just lower that fence, we'd be in a position to see *them*. We'd see who they are. We'd see what they like, who they're becoming, and what they're up to.

The worst that we can do, is raise this fence on ourselves. We expect so much of ourselves. We've raised this fence so high that all we can see is what we haven't achieved, what we haven't done, where we've fallen short, and where we've failed. In the process, we miss everything that we have done. And since we can't see it and don't notice it, we can't value it, appreciate it, or love it.

We have so often failed to truly love ourselves, our kids, and our spouses because of the expectation fences that we've built. Our challenge is to lower those fences so we can see them, appreciate them, and love them! Here's what that looks like.

I'm a guy. I tend to leave a trail of things behind me that I carelessly don't think to put away. My farts stink. I snore at night. My wife reminds me constantly that I'm a guy. But when she lowers her fence, she can see me on the other side. She can see what I am doing: How I'm helping with the kids, or fixing broken stuff, or working hard to support us. She hugs me, gives me a kiss, and tells me that she appreciates me because she can see everything I'm doing. I feel like a superhero! When I feel seen, valued, appreciated, and loved, it inspires me to do even more! It inspires me to work harder, to be aware of my shortcomings instead of defending them, to think of creative ways that I can be even better to her.

When my wife sees the glass of her marriage as half-full, and focuses on what she has instead of what she doesn't, it inspires me to do more and be better! When you see the glass of your job as half-full and you're focused on the good that it offers you position yourself to get the attention of your boss and pursue a greater role! If you sit around and whine about how bad everything is, your wife, your boss, or your kids, aren't going to be inspired to put in more effort to help you. They're going to start feeling really bummed when you're around. If you can't be grateful for what you already have, you'll never get more!

If you see the glass as half-empty, you are welcome to call yourself a realist! However, you better realistically get used to being average. If you want to achieve big things, you need to be a powerful optimist who sees giants as enemies to slay and hurdles as obstacles to overcome! When we see the glass as half-full, our focus is on what we have. We're positive, appreciative, and excited! We're positioned to value, appreciate, and love ourselves and others. But how we see that glass doesn't have much to do with us at all. It has everything to do with the company we keep.

 If you want to achieve big things, you need to be a powerful optimist who sees giants as enemies to slay and hurdles as obstacles to overcome.

You're moving your life in a new direction. You're making powerful decisions to believe in an amazing future. You're going to need to tell people! I have heard it a dozen times that in attitude, finances, relationships, and life we are the average of the five people we spend the most time with. If we are surrounded by people who see the glass as half empty, focus on what they don't have, and raise fences of expectation around everyone they know until nobody can earn their affection, then we are going to get sucked into that same trap.

When we open our mouths and declare our new vision, our dream, our inevitable success, but are surrounded by people who call themselves realists, they are going to doubt, and fear, and smear their disbelief all over our dreams. Realists see statistics as predetermined fate. They will attempt to talk you out of anything that appears statistically difficult to achieve no matter how great it may be. With company like that, we are going to have a much harder time building the belief necessary to achieve those dreams.

If we are going to build the required belief in ourselves and the inevitability of our success, then we are going to have to cut ties with the realists in our lives, and surround ourselves instead with powerful optimists who encourage us, believe in us, support us, and celebrate us! There are going to be relationships that no longer serve the new you. You're going to have to create that distance so you can open yourself to new, amazing relationships! Some of the relationships you'll have to cut ties with will be close to you, and it will be hard. They may not understand. You don't have to do it in a mean way at all, but you have to do it!

The longer you remain surrounded by relationships that aren't supporting your vision, the longer you are limiting your vision to the scope of other people. We cannot set our goals and create our vision of what we want based on how likely other people think we are to achieve it. When you step boldly out to rock the boat, and start moving in a new direction, it will unnerve people! They will think you've lost your mind. They will tell you how improbable and unlikely your dream is to ever come true. They will tell you horror stories of sailors who struck out on their own and got lost at sea. You will have your haters, but you can't cater to the hater. You can't limit your goals and your vision and your story to the scope of their beliefs. The foundation supports the destination. Just because their foundation is insecure, weak, and cannot support the weight of something big and awesome, doesn't mean you have to scale back!

Achieving great things against all the odds and statistics and obstacles in your way is hard! Doing it surrounded by people who constantly build your doubt instead of your resolve is almost impossible! You don't need to be statistically average, so go be great!

Step I is simple:

"Want something."

Step II is simple:

"Believe you *can* achieve what you want"

Step III is simple:

"Believe you are *worthy* of achieving what

you want"

Step IV is simple:

"Believe you *will* achieve what you want"

Post Chapter Questionnaire:

Question 1: Who are the 5 people you spend the most time with? Are their lives an example of where you want your life to be?

Question 2: Do you think these people will believe in you and your dream? Support you? Encourage you? Celebrate you? Or will they doubt you? Minimize or ignore your success? Make believing harder?

Question 3: Make a list of 10 reasons your life, your kids, your spouse, your job are awesome! Focusing on what you have and why it's great is imperative to keep a grateful and positive spirit, which is the only way you can position yourself for greater things. If you're not grateful for what you already have, you'll never get more.

Chapter V:

#TakingBackYourStory

"A fear is just a lie that you've rehearsed so many times you believe it's true." -Robin Sharma- Canadian author, motivational speaker, and ass-kicker.

"The reason we struggle with insecurity is because we compare our behind the scenes with everyone else's highlight reel" -Steven Furtik, American pastor, author, speaker of life

There's a beauty in being an artist that most people never realize. The ability to take a soggy lump of brown clay, or a blank canvas, or an instrument, or a page, or a giant chunk of granite and turn it into something that previously only ever existed in one's head is perhaps the most like God we'll ever be. For most of us, and this is the category where I live, the stuff in my head stays there because my attempts to turn it from thought to reality get lost in translation.

"NO, Jim, STUPID!!! There are 5 fingers, dammit, and why is the head so big? Stupid art. And that stupid poem doesn't even rhyme cool-looking hipster guy. I mean, seriously, anybody? What's the point of a poem that doesn't rhyme? It's called a short story. Pshhh...artists."

My personal attempts at creation always look better in my head than they do when I turn it into reality, so I've learned to kind of stick to what I'm good at, which is decidedly not art. And while I love to cook, and I'm quite good at it, I'm not a chef. A chef creates the recipe from nothing. I'm a cook. I follow instructions well, but I don't create.

A lot of us approach life like the cook instead of the chef. We can follow directions. We find mentors, coaches, and people we admire, and we do our best to imitate them. In fact, the imitation of people we admire does a lot to affirm and validate our decisions. After all, if these admirable people are doing it, no one can point to us and think we're weird, or abnormal, or crazy, because we can just point to the person we're following.

This basic psychological understanding is the entire premise behind the advertising strategy of getting celebrity endorsements for products. If they're using it, doing it, driving it, eating it, then I'm safe to try it, because I won't be alone. We're social creatures who find a natural safety in numbers. We learn this early on in grade school in our seemingly life-or-death struggle to fit in and not be viewed as a "Sweat Pants Master," an out cast, a weirdo. As long as we're not first to do anything, and the person we're following is widely respected, then we find comfort in pursuing it.

Few people have the courage to be the first. Nobody wants to put their neck on the chopping block to just see what happens. How do you think our ancestors learned which mushrooms they could eat and which ones to avoid? They didn't have chemical analysis from modern laboratories. They watched Uncle Ralph try it. When he turned ashy, started frothing at the mouth, and never woke up, they looked at each other and said, "Hey guys!!! Add the medium sized brown one with black spots to the don't eat list. That one actually takes you down quick. You should have seen Uncle Ralph, it was pretty gross."

Think about your large purchases or big decisions: that timeshare in Myrtle Beach, your certified pre-owned Nissan Altima, the move out west to Denver to pursue an opportunity, the 70-inch 4K TV in the room so small you can't back far enough away to take it all in at once, quitting your job to pour your time into a dream you'd always regret not pursuing, your pontoon party boat with built-in LED lighting, etc. We post pics on FB and Instagram, offer to drive so people can see the car, invite people to the lake to enjoy the boat, host the crew for the big game, all because we're looking for validation. We're looking for people to affirm the decision we made. We wrestled over that decision. We were on the fence. And now that we pulled the trigger, we're putting it all out there so that the praise we attract will affirm that we made the right choice.

But what if we could live boldly? What if we weren't scared to be first? What if we were so confident in ourselves, that we could blaze trails, invite people to come with us, and laugh off the people who ever doubted us? What if our vision was so big for who we were and where we were going that we could take a blank page and write an amazing story of power, choice, victory, success, love, and fulfillment? What if the story we wrote with our lives emboldened our children, and their children to pursue their dreams with a wild abandon, all because you inspired them to truly live life to the fullest?

The story you write with your life will impact your children, and their children. The only question is: Are you writing like an artist? Boldly to creating, molding, sculpting, painting, and designing something powerfully beautiful? Or are you a cook, staying in the lines laid out for you, using the color palette you were told to, staring at the model you're trying desperately to recreate?

You weren't designed to follow anyone's lead. The DNA combination that fused in your mother's womb is so unique that there has never been, in all of human history, that exact combination before. There couldn't have been! It literally took all of human history up until now to create the genetic information that made you. You are a marvel of

123

humanity. You are unique. There has never been, and will never be another you. Your job is to be as *you* as you can be.

Your job is to be alive to your passion: What excites you? Your job is to be aware of your skill set: What are you good at? And your job is to fight, with all the strength of your being, to resist the temptation to compare yourself to anyone else. You are not them. You are not supposed to be them. You can't be them. The harder you try, the more you look like a poor chef's underpaid line cook, or a cheap imitation knock-off of an original. The shame of it all is you're robbing the world of their only chance to see *you*. You're robbing yourself of the chance to *be* you. You're robbing your spouse, your kids, and your family the chance to know you, because you're writing someone else's story with your life.

We write a story everyday with our lives, and that story determines whether we are fulfilled or filled with regret. Your children are watching you write that story, the same way you watched your parents write their stories. They're even learning how to write their own story by watching you. Are you going to write for them (and for yourself) a powerful story of intentionality, or are you going to hand your story over to fear?

Are you going to write a story of overcoming obstacles to achieve goals, or are you giving your story over to insecurity?

"Gosh, I really want to go to law school, but I don't even know how to begin. It all seems so overwhelming, I'm so busy already, here you go INSECURITY, you can write this chapter for me. I'll be over here, behind the bar, working for tips, while you write."

We do this all the time. We hand our story over to fear, doubt, insecurity, and circumstances, and allow them the power to write chapters for us while we float mindlessly through life. Some people wake up, and say, *"WHOA! What happened?!?! This is not the life I wanted. I never would have chosen this for myself."*

And then they go out and have an affair, or buy a convertible, or spend their life savings on a luxury trip to Greece, just to feel alive! We know of this great awakening by the name "Mid-Life Crisis." It's usually marked by passionate and utterly irresponsible decisions as a reaction to a life lived without excitement or intentionality. What's terribly un-funny is that this is so common we almost expect it. None of us even seem to be certain which is worse: Waking up and acting irresponsibly to make up for lost time, or never waking up at all

Fortunately, those aren't your only options. You can wake up now! You can take back your story from fear, doubt, insecurity, and circumstances and start driving your life rather than drifting. You can start flying instead of floating.

You can live a life by design instead of default. It's not too late. But it's going to take some work.

We are all witnesses to amazing stories being written every single day! From well-known ones like Mother Teresa, Will Smith, and Steve Jobs, to the countless numbers of people overcoming incredible odds to start charities and businesses and lead organizations that are changing the world. How can some people seemingly take over the world while the rest of us have trouble taking over a single afternoon? Why have some people accomplished more with their day before 8 a.m. than others of us will accomplish in a week? How does that guy look so good and dress so well just to drop his kids off at the elementary school, and I'm in the same drop-off line in old hospital scrubs and camouflage crocs with sleep lines still embedded on my cheeks? Are they just smarter? Better looking? Did they have an easier road? What separates us?

There's an answer. And the first step to that answer is realizing the cultural lie that is so prevalent that many of us have believed without even being aware. From magazines to billboards, from commercials to political statements, from the mom next door to leading news publications: We are told that it is not our fault.

"You can't help it. It's not your fault. Anyone in your situation would have done the same thing."

"You can't fight genetics. Don't worry about it. Look at what you're up against. You were born this way, you can't help who you are."

"Honey, it's not your fault, there's nothing you could have done about it. You're not responsible for this. You can't help it."

This cultural lie screams out: "Nobody can help anything, and we're all just victims riding a conveyor belt of comfort, and everybody's okay".

ALL. LIES.

Unless you want to believe them. See, on the surface, it may sound so nice and cozy.

"HOLY CRAP! If it's not my fault, doesn't that take the weight off my shoulders!"

"If I can't help it, then I can't be held responsible."

"If I'm a victim of my circumstances, then there's nothing I can do."

"If I'm born this way, then I might as well just accept my fate."

"If there's nothing I could do about it, don't I get to just rest in that knowledge and give up fighting?"

Yes. You can rest in that knowledge, and you can rest in that comfort to your grave. You'll never move forward. And you'll never achieve anything.

The people who are writing successful stories with their lives don't believe any of that. People who are kicking

People who are kicking ass know that they can't always control their circumstances, but they also know that their results in life depend on their response to circumstances, not the circumstances themselves.

ass know that they can't always control their circumstances, but they also know that their results in life depend on their response to circumstances, not the circumstances themselves.

The minute you believe you are powerless to respond to circumstances, you are powerless. The minute you believe and understand that you have the power to control how you react to circumstances, that is the same moment you have the power to change your story. You can take back your story from circumstance, fear, doubt, and insecurity, and you can start writing the story of a champion! You can write a story of recognizing obstacles, but not giving in to them. You can write one of setting goals, and achieving them. You can write a story of kicking ass!

People who are winning at life have what others don't because they're willing to do what others won't! All of nature follows the path of least resistance. We see this watching water flowing down a creek, or following deer on a path through the woods. All of nature is looking for the easiest route. The difference between a remarkable story, and our everyday average story is the choice we make between comfort or challenge.

You're going to face that choice 1,000 times per day. You're going to face it when that alarm goes off in the morning. You're going to face it when your kids are yelling at you. You're going to face it when you see the escalator and the stairs side by side. You're going to face it staring at the menu and choosing between the greasy cheeseburger with fries or lean salad with dressing on the side. You're going to face it on Black Friday when you either fight to be in line at 1 a.m. or you go to bed and let others get the deals. You're going to face it in the evening when you're exhausted and you'd rather binge watch Netflix with a bottle of red than sit down and intentionally re-work your resume. Successful people have what others don't, because they're willing to do what others won't.

Every time you choose comfort, you're believing the lie that you are powerless to affect real change in your life. Every time you choose comfort, you are giving your story away, and you are going to stay comfortable. Like everybody else. And that's fine, but there's nothing remarkable in that. You're going to drift through life and wonder why everybody else has what you want.

If you want your story to be remarkable, if you want your story to be a legacy story of overcoming, of power, of success, of fulfillment, you are going to choose challenge.

When that alarm goes off in the morning, you're not going to hit snooze. You're going to get up. Getting up is just a little bit harder. When dinner's over and the kids are going crazy and you're exhausted from a long day at work and the noise is overwhelming? It's easy to pour a glass of wine and collapse on the couch. It's a little harder to grab a glass of water and pound out 30 minutes on the elliptical. It's a littler harder. But every time you choose challenge over comfort, you get a little stronger. Every time you choose challenge, it gets a little easier.

Every time you choose challenge you are rejecting the mindless drift of least resistance. You are getting comfortable being uncomfortable, and that is going to position you for success. That is going to separate you from ordinary and position you to start being extraordinary.

What do we do, though, if all of this sounds great, but we just actually can't get ourselves to do it? What if we are following all the steps: We want something (chapter 1), we believe that we can get it (chapter 2), that we are worthy of it (chapter 3), and that we will achieve it (chapter 4)…but when it comes to actually putting one foot in front of the other, we remain frozen? What do we do then? How do we actually take back our story from the fear of failure and rejection, the fear of success, or the fear of putting ourselves out there and declaring our dream? How do we take our stories back from insecurity, and doubt, and circumstances?

Take back your story from Fear:

I had a coaching call with Amanda earlier this year. She was an insurance adjustor for years before starting her own business as a franchisee with a premium skincare company. Early returns on her business were so promising that she replaced her income and was able to leave her day job and stay home with her two young kiddos. The structure of her business added to that flexibility by operating exclusively through an online storefront so she didn't have to physically keep hours, or maintain a traditional brick-and-mortar location.

But those early returns that showed such a promising trajectory slowed to a grinding halt in the subsequent year. She was still earning a residual income from her loyal customer base, but wasn't generating any new business. However, our coaching call wasn't a trouble-shooting call. We both knew where the trouble was: FEAR. She knew what she wanted and had the destination on lock. She knew how to get there and the vehicle's manual memorized. But when the driver is scared, it doesn't matter how well they know how to operate the vehicle.

Her early success fit right into her comfort zone. She did what any entrepreneur does when they open a business: Tell all of their friends, family, and biggest supporters and have a fun launch party. That initial excitement drove a lot of volume! The product line delivered on its claims, so the initial volume became residual volume, and initial customers became loyal customers. But now she was facing an obstacle: "How do I reach out to people beyond my existing network? How do I promote my business and this brand? How do I introduce people to this? How do I bring it up in conversation, or advertise it, or promote it?" And it's not that she didn't have answers to those questions. She knew exactly how to do all of those things. But she couldn't get herself to do them. She couldn't talk about her business because she was concerned with what people would think. She worried that people would assume her business was weird for operating online instead of in a store. What if people thought that the product line was too expensive? What if they said no, and rejected her?

Once the growth of her business depended on taking action outside of her comfort zone, she froze. Her business plateaued, and she gave her story away to fear. This isn't unique. This story is so common, we might call it normal. I'll quote Jen Sincero again: *"Most of us never decide. We sign up to try until it gets too uncomfortable."* That was certainly happening here. If Amanda's business was going to move forward, she was going to have to step outside of her comfort zone.

If you're going to have something you've never had, you're going to have to do something you've never done!

And that is going to require stepping outside of your comfort zone and taking your story back from fear. But if we're going to do that, then we need to understand what fear actually is.

At its very basic core, fear is simply biochemical feedback that says, "Hey, ummm…you might want to avoid this action/scenario/place/person that has potentially devastating circumstances. Remember Uncle Ralph? Not those mushrooms, dude, not those mushrooms."

Except fear doesn't speak in such a measured tone. Fear makes the hair stand up on the back of our necks. It turns our stomachs to knots, and we get a rush that screams: "Run, you FREAKING IDIOT!!!! GO GO GO…DO NOT PASS GO!! DO NOT COLLECT $200…GET THE &*%$ OUT OF HERE!!!!!" We know fear to be useful because it keeps us from doing stupid crap that can hurt us. Fear instructs us to avoid.

However, fear only instructs us to avoid. Fear never says, "*GO FOR IT!*". Fear never says, *"How high can you climb?"*. Fear never says, *"Hey Jerry, hold my beer and watch this."* Fear never tells us to run into the burning building, or to chase the lion, to ask out the girl, or to walk back into the school dance after climbing out of the dumpster. Fear only instructs us to avoid. And while that can be useful, way too often, we don't use fear wisely!

We simply forget that fear is a tool. It's like an advisor. It provides input, but we still choose the direction.

We can choose to take fear's advice or not to. We forget that. So often we elevate fear to the position of God, and, with shaking knees, we feel as though we have to listen. This is how we turn our story over to fear. We forget that fear serves us, not the other way around.

Once we elevate fear and start serving it, we give it unchallenged access to our minds, hearts, souls, and vision. It then grows like an aggressive tumor, and once we've given our story over to it, it stops being an advisor and starts running the show. It stops giving suggestions that you can choose to take or not, and it starts issuing commands that you feel powerless to challenge. It stops simply advising you to avoid situations with known negative outcomes, and it starts commanding you to avoid situations altogether that simply have unknown outcomes. Simply put, instead of just avoiding crap that's going to hurt us, we start avoiding everything that has an unknown outcome.

Rather than walking boldly into the unknown, we retreat to our routines that are safe and comfortable. Rather than promoting our business, we retreat to safety and comfort, and settle for a plateau. Rather than talk with our family about the elephant in the room, we retreat to safety and comfort and allow unhealthy relationship habits to continue. Rather than tell someone our dreams, we retreat, and keep them bottled up inside. Rather than push for a raise because we've taken on more responsibility and are adding more value to the company, we retreat to safety and comfort and go to work feeling undervalued.

We constantly retreat to safety and comfort, and we learn to love them so much, that we learn to fear being uncomfortable. With fear in charge, any time our comfort zone is threatened, we have a million little red flags that go off as a warning, and yell to us, "Whoa! CRAZYTOWN! You can't go do THAT!!! That will take you away from this comfortable, cozy, safe place we've worked so hard to build together! I mean, you could be scammed! People might reject you! Mexico is totally unsafe this time of year! Your boss probably won't be happy if you ask for that raise! You can't seriously be thinking of meeting this guy, right? He could be a total creeper!"

And let's talk about what we're afraid of, because it's never the thing we think. We're not afraid of heights like we say we are; we're afraid of falling. We're not afraid of sharks; we're afraid of getting eaten alive. We're not afraid of snakes; we're afraid of the scale-y nasty things wrapping around our arms and swallowing our hands. We're not afraid of talking to people; we're afraid of being rejected. We're not afraid of commitment; we're afraid of getting hurt. We're not afraid of succeeding; we're afraid of the judgement that our families throw at successful people. We're not afraid of the actual thing, we're afraid of the negative consequences we associate with that thing.

But so often, we just use our powerful imaginations to make up the negative consequences we fear. It's a defense mechanism we use to justify running away. Since we have no idea what the consequences would be, we start making up bad ones and running away from stuff that is at best extremely unlikely and at worst completely imaginary! The process goes like this:

- This is uncomfortable.

- I'm scared.

- I want to run away.

- Let's make up some reasons that sound good.

This is actually what happens in your brain without consulting your conscious mind at all.

When we start allowing the fear of unknown and unlikely consequences to govern our actions, we start running away from things that just as easily might have amazing outcomes! We could, instead, invent potential positive consequences and run toward it! I had a coach tell me, "If you're going to make it up, make it up good!"

Instead of all the potential negative talk, what if we spoke to ourselves like this:

"Maybe that isn't scam, but an incredible opportunity. Doesn't hurt just to get the info, does it?"

"Maybe people won't reject me, maybe they'll think I'm awesome!"

"Maybe that whole 'Mexico is unsafe' meme is overblown, and I'm going to create a lifetime of memories!"

"Maybe my boss has been thinking about giving me a raise already, he's just too busy to initiate the conversation."

"Maybe that guy is hilarious and awesome, and I'm going to meet the love of my life!"

If we're going to take our story back from fear, we have to challenge the comfort and safety that we've come to so dearly appreciate. Kids don't have that challenge. They're kids. They barely have a routine to retreat to. They're not experts at anything. They're always trying new things. They're always putting themselves out there. They're not afraid to look dumb or to fall, or to fail; they're learning, and everyone knows they're learning. No one expects them to look competent, because they're kids and everything is brand new to them.

But as adults, we don't like to look or feel incompetent. We don't like to fail. We hate to look as if we have no idea what we're doing. We dread feeling as though we don't belong. For that reason, we naturally avoid uncomfortable situations. The problem, if you want to kick ass at life, is that any new situation is always uncomfortable. As a defense mechanism, to avoid feeling uncomfortable, we end up avoiding all things new. Through avoidance, we settle into routines that run our lives on a comfortable autopilot.

I remember my first day in the ICU as a registered nurse. I had been a nurse on the step down unit for a couple years and had developed a good rapport. My reputation earned me a position in the ICU, and this required me to learn a ton of new crap! Lab results, procedures, medications, machines, trusting intuition, monitoring equipment and parameters, etc. I was no longer helping patients heal from a single procedure, I had to be aware of how each and every little thing affected each and every other little thing. I learned to see the body as a whole and completely interdependent unit.

I walked into the ICU on that very first day and met my preceptor. She was the experienced nurse that I had been set up to shadow for a few weeks until I got the hang of things. She walked me into our patient's room, and my eyes nearly jumped out of my head! There were 13 continuous intravenous infusions pumping through machines at different rates all at the same time. Any of these had the potential to kill the patient. There was a machine at the foot of the bed feeding a catheter into the patient's groin. This machine was inflating and deflating a balloon inside the aorta, and it also had the potential to kill the patient. There was another machine at the head of the bed with tubes attached to a plastic piece down the throat to breathe for the patient. Also potentially fatal. Yet another machine connected to catheters coming from the chest, and this one took out all of the their blood, filtered it, and sent it back to the body; and yes, it could totally kill the patient.

I remember thinking to myself, *"I will never be able to wrap my mind around everything that is happening in this room!"* The machines all need to be monitored, and constantly adjusted according to lab results or numbers on the screen. Each machine and each medication has different potential negative consequences that we needed to be vigilant to watch for…constantly. There were flashing lights and alarms, and some of them were incredibly important while others meant nothing. I thought, *"Maybe I could learn one of the machines, or a few of the medications,"* but this was so far over my head that I was legitimately terrified! What had I gotten myself into? Why did I think this job was a good idea? How was I ever going to learn all of this?

That first day was overwhelmingly uncomfortable for reasons like: I felt insecure, incompetent, I worried my co-workers would reject me, I felt like I didn't belong, I felt as though I might accidentally kill someone. However, I went back the next day, and the day after that, and the day after that. While I was afraid of uncharted territory, I knew the only way to get over it was to actually chart the territory.

It took me a year to truly get comfortable. By that anniversary mark, however, I was competent and trusted to care for any patient who came through the ICU door. What was at one time terrifying and uncomfortable became comfortable, but only because I continued to show up instead of retreating.

If we are going to take our stories back from fear, we are going to have to give fear a demotion from God to advisor. When fear tells us, "STOP, RUN AWAY!", we're not going to blindly listen. Instead, we're going to ask why.

"Why should I run? What's the worst that could happen?"

"How likely is it that the negative consequences I fear are actually going to occur?"

I had forgotten this trick when we were visiting Cave of the Winds and I ran away from the Terror-Dactyl. Fear told me to run because I was worried that the cable might break, and I might plummet to my death tied to a two-seater chair. I listened to fear and ran before rationally understanding no one had ever fallen and the ride was actually very safe. I had run from an incredibly unlikely scenario that my imagination invented.

When we got home from that trip and actually had internet service, we Googled "Terror-Dactyl" and got to watch videos of 90-year-old women and kids on YouTube enjoying the ride like it was a hoot! I hadn't avoided a terrifying death. I had missed out on a thrillingly exciting experience.

Fear tells us to run away. It's a great advisor, but a terrible God.

In my call with Amanda, we pin-pointed that her fear wasn't actually marketing her business, it was two-fold: It was a fear of not knowing what to say in conversation (a fear of appearing incompetent) and a fear of rejection rolled into one.

These dual fears of incompetence and rejection held her captive. She was running away from any opportunity to promote a business that had been amazing both for herself and her customers. We started asking questions in an effort to demote her fear to advisor status:

"Amanda, you're afraid to talk to people about your product line because you're not sure what to say. What is the worst that could possibly happen if you entered into a conversation with somebody and found yourself at a true loss for words, or mumbled, or stuttered, or completely bombed your elevator pitch?

"Well," she replied, "I would break out in red splotches and they'd think I was dumb, and they'd say no to purchasing."

"Are you certain they would think you were dumb, or would you just feel dumb?"

She conceded, "Well, I wouldn't know what they were actually thinking, so I guess I would just feel dumb."

"Is there a chance they might even resonate with your discomfort? Or not even notice it?"

"Sure, I guess it's possible.

I went on, "Okay, what's the result you're currently experiencing from not talking to people?"

"Ummm…well, I'm feeling dumb, I'm getting angry at myself, I'm breaking out in red splotches, and nobody new is purchasing."

"Okay, and finally, what's the best scenario that could happen if you talked to somebody?"

She answered, "Well, I could land a client who loved the product, and in turn helped me promote it. And my business would grow, and I'd open up more options for my two kids."

In her case, the negative consequences she feared were already occurring, and she had nowhere to go but up. Once she could realize the irrationality of her fear, she could act intentionally in spite of it.

Chances are, your fear is irrational also. Either the consequences that you're running away from are completely made up or extremely unlikely. In either case, the reward from acting in spite of your fear, taking back your story, and overcoming will be far greater!

Take your story back from Insecurity

This past year I ran a fitness coaching course based on the simple premise that the recipe for success is the same whether you apply it to business, fitness, relationships, or finances. I had achieved tremendous success in business using these principles, so I decided to bet that they would translate to the fitness world seamlessly.

While I knew the value of the coaching program would truly help people reach their goals even when nothing else could, I had to unpack some deep insecurity myself. In 2003 I ran a marathon in 3 hours and 21 minutes. I looked good. I was fast. I felt amazing. I met a beautiful girl. I got married. I got a job, built a business, had 3 amazing kids, and got busy. We were always moving! We had checklists, to do lists, laundry lists, and in the blur of the last 12 years, I forgot to take care of me!

I had officially gained 60 pounds over 12 years (which for the math nerds, is a very simple 5 pounds per year), and while I had done a ton of awesome things during that time, taking care of myself was not one of them. While I knew I could truly help people, I wondered: "Who was going to take fitness advice from a 260 pound coach?" I wrestled with my value. I allowed my insecurity to cloud my vision. I didn't feel good enough, strong enough, or brave enough.

I've been blessed in my life to know some amazingly successful, and powerful people. I know some people who light up a room, that are brilliant, fun, funny, and rich. These are the kind of people you simply want to be around. But as powerful as they seem to others, on the inside, they wrestle with the same thoughts we all do: *"I'm fat, I'm shy, my wife seems distant, these stretch marks look terrible, I'm not smart enough for this project and people are going to notice, my house is a mess, my kids don't like me, I can't stop smoking, etc."*

It boggles my mind how people who can appear to be so put together on the outside, have the same struggles we all do on the inside. But these insecurities are lies.

Insecurity is just a matter of allowing past failures to determine present reality. You're literally allowing your past to determine your present. Maybe, like me, you're overweight, and it didn't happen overnight. You've started to define yourself by this over the years, to the degree you now call yourself "fat" and identify yourself as a "fat person". You don't simply see this as a passing phase of life — you've allowed it to actually define your life.

But let me tell you what I've learned to see. When you look in the mirror and you see 40 pounds overweight, I see a beautiful person who is in a phase of life where something other than fitness has captured their attention, time, and energy. While you are beating yourself up and defining yourself by your "failure," I'm seeing success. Maybe instead of going to the gym and running everyday, you've been going to night classes, doing the laundry, making dinners and lunches, helping with homework, and ensuring you have happy, well-adjusted kids in a peaceful home. Where you see an overweight failure, I see a rockstar mom who chose to give her children and family the best of her time and creative energy! The extra weight was simply the cost of creating an amazing home with happy kids. That's a badge to wear proudly, not a dunce-cap of shame!

Every single thing we choose to do in the whole world comes at the cost of something else that we could be doing with that same time. I'm aware that includes reading this book, which is why I'm humbled and honored with each note of appreciation I get, because I recognize that you could have done any number of other things with your time. So when we choose to do one thing, it inevitably means that something else didn't get done. Why then, do we choose to look at what we haven't done, instead of what we have done? Why are we judging ourselves by what we've not accomplished, instead of by what we've actually been hugely successful with? Stop looking at what you're not doing, and instead, give yourself credit for what you are doing.

You haven't been a failure; you haven't even failed. In fact, to the opposite, you've been incredibly successful, you just haven't been giving yourself credit for the things you've done! We all understand that success comes at a cost: "No pain, no gain," right? You're going to drop something in order to achieve something.

But what we don't often understand is that the opposite is also true! Every "failure," every "dropped ball," every "falling short," every "defeat," came at the cost of achieving success somewhere else! Stop seeing your failures as an ultimate judgement against yourself and start looking at them as an indication of success. You can't fail something without succeeding somewhere else.

So, instead of saying, "Uggghhh, I suck at keeping up with this laundry. I cannot keep this stupid room organized." Start saying, "Huh, this laundry room is a mess, I must be spending my time doing other things. What have I done awesomely instead of the laundry?" Instead of looking in the mirror and thinking, "This shirt looks horrible, the buttons are spreading apart, I think I can see my belly hair in between the buttons. I can't get in shape!" Start thinking, "Hmmm, I've put on a few pounds. Clearly I'm not paying attention to what I'm eating, so what has been getting my attention instead?"

And while we're learning to reframe our thinking, let's take it one step further. See, most of our insecurities come from comparison. If we lived all by ourselves, and had no standard, or no one to judge ourselves against, we'd probably be pretty happy. But what do we do? We go on Facebook, and we see that PTA mom who's 5'9" and 130 pounds. Her physical beauty is clearly a success, and we turn and judge her single public success against our failure. We see the guy on the fantasy football team show up to the draft in his Land Rover, and we're pretty sure the payments on that thing are more than the rent we have trouble affording. We compare his success with our failure.

We're not comparing their failure against our failure. We're not comparing their success against our success. We're not even giving ourselves the benefit of the doubt and comparing our own success to their failure. We are only comparing their success to our failure. We only ever judge the failures and weaknesses we know of ourselves with the successes we see in others.

We have no idea the cost they paid for the success we see. Maybe PTA mom has struggled with an eating disorder and the cost of her 130 pounds has been an unhealthy relationship with food, and she's had to carry the baggage of anorexia for the last 10 years. Maybe fantasy football guy has been divorced twice and is alienated from his kids because he spent all his time at work chasing money and success and promotion. The success we see came at a huge cost!

It's very easy for us to see other people's successes, but we can't always see the price they paid for it. There is always a cost. So stop comparing yourself to other people, because you don't know the price they paid for the success you see. If you knew, you might not even think it was worth it. And to top it off, you don't know if they even think it was worth it. You don't know the demons they carry in their closets. You don't realize that they look at you on Facebook and are jealous of the happy family that you've been so successful at cultivating.

If we're going to take back our stories from insecurity, we're going to have to start realizing that we are successful, powerful, and awesome! I moved forward with my fitness coaching course and had 93 people enroll! The feedback was absolutely amazing. People who had tried everything to lose weight felt empowered, excited, and reached goals that they had started to wonder if they would ever be able to reach. The power I had within me to coach people to success would never have touched these lives if I had allowed the insecurity of my weight gain to define my value.

 Failures don't define you; they simply describe your priorities.

Failures don't define you; they simply describe your priorities. I gained weight, not because I'm a failure; I gained it because I was busy being an awesome dad, and husband, and growing a great business! There were other things at that phase of my life that were more important to me. The "failure" of weight gain didn't define me, it simply described my priorities. When you look at your life and you see "failure," STOP IT! Realize that there are other things that are simply more important to you, and you've been spending your time on those things.

I want us to go so far as to realize that every failure is a banner that actually proclaims our success! I mentioned earlier how my mom was valedictorian of her high school and her college and top in her med school class. My grandfather and uncle are certified genius. My dad was an incredibly successful student, earning a master's with high honors while working full time to support a family. So when I went to college, it was expected that I was going to be awesome!

I had all the tools in the toolbox to take our family's academic legacy to the next level, and nearly every semester I came home with a C (ish) transcript. I think I had like a 2.1 GPA a few semesters. HOLY CRAP! What was wrong? My parents would try to trouble shoot. At times they tried to shame me, and give me a "failure" label, but I refused to accept it. I was busy building incredible relationships with incredible people who I knew were going to be far more important both in the present and foreseeable future than any particular grade. You couldn't pin failure on me, because I knew that failure was really a banner proclaiming my success.

When someone tries to tell you that you're too big, too slow, too ugly, too disorganized, you're going to see a banner of success! When someone looks at you and says,

"You turned your back and let this whole thing fall apart," you're going to look right back at them and say, "You're right, I did turn my back. But walk in my shoes for a minute. Come with me, let me show you what I built instead."

"How can you live with your garage looking like this?"

"Oh, GOSH, I can live with that so easily! Come here, let me show you this fun game I invented with the kids that I've been playing instead."

"WOW! You really let yourself go, 40 pounds? Really?"

"Yeah. Forty pounds. Happened pretty quick, too, but come over here and check out this business proposal I've put together that's going to change the trajectory of my family's entire future!"

You are winning. You are powerful. You are absolutely successful. And when you learn to judge yourself by your successes and stop comparing yourself to others you'll be in a position to finally take your story back from the insecurity that has been writing chapters for you while sit on the sideline feeling too inadequate to move toward your dream.

Step I is simple:

"Want something."

Step II is simple:

"Believe you *can* achieve what you want"

Step III is simple:

"Believe you are *worthy* of achieving what

you want"

Step IV is simple:

"Believe you *will* achieve what you want"

Step V is simple:

"Take back your story"

Post Chapter Questionnaire:

Question 1: How would you describe your story so far? Have you been writing it, or have you been giving it away?

Question 2: When you decline an invitation, or an opportunity, or drive away from the Terror-Dactyl, or choose not to have the tough conversation, are you running away because you're scared, or because it's wise? Running away or saying no to an opportunity isn't always bad but we need to make sure that the consequences we fear are both real and likely. Initially, our fear can often be too blinding and we may need a third party to help us weight the pros and cons. My hope is that we'll get to a place where we are making decisions based on opportunity and not fear.

Question 3: While you've been beating yourself up for your failures, you've actually been achieving some pretty incredible things that you're likely not giving yourself credit for. What are these things? Where have you been investing your time and what's come of it? Maybe the only success you can name is your rockstar online status with video games. That's okay! A conversation on priorities and whether the things you're doing will get you to your goal is a much easier conversation when you recognize your ability to actually be really good at something! Maybe you've split your time among so many things that you've become a jack-of-all-trades, but master at none. That's okay, too! Recognize that, and give yourself credit for being more well-rounded than many of your peers!

Question 4: The goal of marketing is to make a product or service sound appealing. Most marketing campaigns aren't intentionally misleading, they're just intentionally focused on the positive attributes. Often, those positive attributes come at the cost of other positive attributes. For example: "Luxury materials" usually comes at the cost of "affordable." "Great flavor" often comes at the cost of "good for you." With a lot of cell phones, "thin design" means "short battery life." No product, service, or person offers everything! It's high time you write down a list of the amazing things you offer to sell yourself to yourself, not ignoring the weaknesses, but understanding that those weaknesses were the cost of achieving your incredible strengths!

Part III

The Vehicle

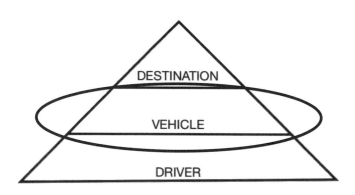

The vehicle is the actionable plan you utilize to drive toward your destination. It's the diet, the workout regimen, the grad school program, the business coach, etc. We can't get to our destination without a vehicle. While it's not as important as the driver — because a confident driver can mask the deficiencies in a number of vehicles through sheer grit and determination — faith in the vehicle's ability to actually get you there is imperative.

Many people no matter how confident they are in themselves, don't pursue their dreams because they actually have no idea how to get there. They feel stuck. They feel overwhelmed. In short, they lack a vehicle.

Other people jump into vehicles, but never learn to trust them. Results don't happen overnight. If you don't believe in the vehicle to ultimately deliver results, then you're going to bail on it when you don't 'feel' like it's working. This is why people start and stop 100 different diet plans. They have a destination. They may even believe in themselves to be successful. They simply can't find a vehicle they trust to stick with.

Faith in your vehicle is imperative. You have an amazing dream on the horizon, but you don't take a vehicle to the horizon if you don't trust it to get you to the grocery store and back. You're going to have to test drive that vehicle so it can prove itself and you can build your faith in it.

That looks as easy as giving it small goals, working the plan, hitting the goals, and then raising the bar a little. Do that again. As the vehicle proves faithful to deliver results, you'll build your belief in it to take you down the road for the long haul.

Chapter VI:

#EasyStreet

"You don't have to see the whole staircase. Just take the first step." -Dr. Martin Luther King, Jr., American Activist, prophet, gave his life fighting to make dreams come true.

"If you can't do the little things right, you'll never do the big things right." Admiral William H. McRaven, decorated Navy officer, commanded the raid that killed Osama bin Laden, Special Operations badass.

I've known Bob for years. There are two things I know about Bob:

1. He's a smoker.
2. He doesn't want to be a smoker.

I've been a witness to this powerful tension playing out for as long as I've known him. Every few months, he declares that he's done smoking, throws away his cigarettes in a ceremonial triumph, gets laid by his wife, and is back to smoking the very next time I see him.

It's easy to say, "Oh, he obviously doesn't really want to quit, I mean if he really wanted to, then he would. My uncle quit cold turkey. Just like that. Threw 'em away, and never looked back."

The truth is far more complex. And we're a lot more like Bob than we either realize or care to admit. We want things. We might really want things. We might want things so badly that we call our friends, tell them "this time we really mean it", spend thousands of dollars on fancy new equipment, cannonball into the deep end — just to come out the other side two weeks later with a bunch of expensive stuff collecting dust in our garage.

What happened? Why is this not the first time this has happened either?

We get fed up with the messy garage, take an entire weekend to clean it, find money in the budget to rent a storage unit, swear we'll never let it get that bad again, and within a year we're carving walking paths through the junk because we can't see the floor anymore.

Our holiday dress is a size up from last year which was a size up from the year before. We're unhappy looking in the mirror so we set our New Year's resolution, get a great discount at the gym by paying up front for 6 months, and by February we're on the sofa wiping the orange Cheetos stain off our hands and onto the workout shirt that was supposed to be very flattering with the new running shoes.

None of this is because we didn't really want it. We did. Desperately. Just like Bob. But having a big and exciting destination in mind, doesn't mean we believe in the vehicle or have confidence in the driver (ourself) to actually get us there.

Tony Robbins says that every big life change we experience can be traced to a magic moment: that single pivotal moment when we said, "That's ENOUGH!" We draw our line in the sand, plant our flag, determine our course, and refuse to give an inch! Every success we achieve stems from a moment in time where our dissatisfaction drove us to an amazing triumph.

And he's absolutely right! I mean, let's be real, he's Tony Robbins, he didn't get where he is by being wrong. Every big life change can be traced to a magic moment. And while that's true, it perhaps glosses over another important truth: While every life change can be traced to a magic moment, not every magic moment produces life change.

Some of us have experienced 1,000 magic moments. We felt it — for real — the shame, the dissatisfaction, the determination that "something has to give". We meant it. We felt it. It was powerful! It was real! We not only wanted it, we actually needed it. We were determined. We knew it was real this time. It was more real this time than it had ever been before! Yet nothing ultimately came of it.

Was that not a real magic moment? Were we faking those tears? Was our shame just a mirage? Did we not really want it? What happened? As far as real things go in our lives, by every measure, this appeared as real as it gets. What happened?

The answer is actually phenomenally simple. We wanted it, we just didn't do it. There are no end to the superlatives used to describe what separates successful people from unsuccessful people. You can google it or ask Siri. You'll find articles stacked on articles, books stacked on books, opinions on top of opinions. I've had the pleasure of working in a profession where I've gotten to know a lot of people on both sides of that of that equation. I'm convinced that successful people are not smarter, sexier, luckier, or even more ambitious than their unsuccessful counterparts. The only true difference, in a word, between people kicking ass and people floating along is "implementation".

Simply taking action and putting what you already know to good use is more than most people can manage. Most people have all the tools and knowledge that they need, they just can't get themselves to actually do anything with it. It's not a secret that eating half of a pizza and drinking a 6-pack of beer is probably not the healthiest choice, and yet people unhappy with their weight all across the country are going to do that exact thing today! It isn't that they didn't know. It isn't that other, healthier options weren't available. It's just that the knowledge and tools mean nothing without actual implementation. This is the same as having a destination, without the foundation to support it. Wanting without doing is a single moment that accomplishes nothing tangible.

There are really only 4 reasons we don't do it if we legitimately really want it. People may want me to add "too busy" to this list, but that's a reflection of an impotent goal you don't really want. Here are the reasons we don't take action toward things we want:

(A) We want it, but we don't think we can achieve it because we're held back by fear and insecurity, so we never take action.

(B) We want it, but we actually have no idea how to go about getting it, we're overwhelmed, so we never take action, or we take scattered, unproductive action.

(C) We're too proud to start small, so we never take action.

(D) We want it so badly we burn ourselves out with massive, unsustainable action.

As real as that magic moment is, life change never happens in a single moment. It happens in 1,000 moments. It happens in the thousand moments we choose challenge over comfort in a steady march toward a new horizon. That magic moment when you determined to quit drinking was real. The magic moment you swore to end the affair and you broke up with him even though you were back at his apartment the following week was real. The magic moment you flipped off your boss and walked off your job to pursue your dream, even though you ended up a month later working for less money for your boss' competitor, was also real. Those moments were all real. They were magic. And they are necessary if we're going to take back our stories and kick ass at life!

But, while they were magic moments, they were each just a single moment. It might have been a magic moment, but it was still just one moment, and life change never happens in a moment no matter how strong our feelings are in that moment.

The magic moment is necessary: It's STEP ONE in our blueprint to kicking ass at life. It's the "want something". It's the destination that crowns the success triangle we talked about in the foreword. You'll never kick ass without a magic moment. The magic moment is the moment you turn the rudder and steer the ship. It's the moment that you do an about face and look at a new horizon. It's the moment that has you rejecting your current trajectory and positioning yourself on a course; toward a new future, to new results, amazing outcomes. Because of that moment you're headed toward success.

But you haven't gotten anywhere yet. All you've done in that moment is turn the wheel. Sure, you're facing a different direction. Sure, that direction is all sorts of exciting. Just thinking about it, you're giddy like a school boy on a snowy day who just heard school was cancelled. But you haven't yet taken even a single step. If you're going to reach that horizon. If you're going to get the thing you so desperately want, you're going to have to take action… over…and over…and over again. John Maxwell says it this way, "Success is not an event, it's a process, a lifelong journey."

I'm hoping after the last chapter, that you're committed to not allowing fear and insecurity to hold you back from something amazing! You have greatness written in your soul, birthed in your heart, and consuming your mind. You have a passionate purpose to live out, so let's discover it by asking those deep questions about what excites you, and then take action! Fear will only ever cause us to run away from pursuing anything exciting. Insecurity is a lie that whispers to your heart that you can't, or that you're not worth it — but it's a lie, because you can, and you are worth it. In fact, the world needs you to pursue it, because there is no other you. There never has been, and there never will be. Don't rob the world its only chance to experience you! We can't let these petty lies distract us and hold us back from the amazing horizon there for us to achieve!

Another reason we fail to take action is similar to when you walk into your kid's room, and the toys are like 3 layers deep on the floor. It looks like a dirty laundry bomb had gone off, and it spewed toys and clothes everywhere! Drawers are half-open, dripping with shirts and pants that may or may not be disgusting. The bed is actually not even resting on the floor anymore because so much crap is crammed underneath it. The sight of a mess this bad makes you freeze in your tracks! Where do you even start!?!

When things get out of hand, that overwhelmed feeling is common. We might feel confident to get rid of those 10 pounds, but 60!? We might be empowered to ask for a cost of living raise, but to radically pursue life changing income…where would we even start? Go back to school? Open a business? But what business? We don't know how to start a business. We might be able to figure out how to heal the rift with our spouse that started over the location of the garbage can, but to heal it from an affair? There's so much deep hurt and mistrust…where do you even start?

And when we get lost in the size of the battle in front of us, it's overwhelming. Even if we believe in ourselves as the driver, what vehicle could possibly get us that far down the road? It seems so far away! When we're overwhelmed, we start to hear those voices of doubt that are so quick to remind us that we're not up to the task: That we can't, that we're not worth it, that we're too busy anyway. The voices whisper, *"You don't even know how, and you've failed before, so…"*

STOP IT! You're not too busy to live! You're not too busy to pursue a life you want! We always make time for the things that are important, in fact, the viewership numbers of *The Bachelor* prove that we actually make time even for things are aren't important. This last part of the book is designed to get you focused. To get you over your excuses, to help you find a vehicle, get married to a plan, and start executing it faithfully at a high level over time to achieve amazing things!

If you have a dream and literally have no idea how to achieve it, you need to find people who do. You are uniquely powerful, and you are going to put a unique twist on something awesome, but chances are, the awesome thing you're going to do has been done before in some capacity. Maybe it has never beed done as well as you will end up doing it, but it's been done. It's likely never been done exactly the way you're going to do it, but it's been done! Your job is to find someone who's done it.

Facebook group pages are actually an amazing way to do just that. There are group pages upon group pages for virtually every hobby, passion, and dream. There are blogs upon blogs, and books upon books If you have a burning passion to write a book on sustainable gardening, find an expert in gardening and an expert in writing. If you want to fill your house with music and learn the piano, find a teacher! If you want to lose weight and you have no idea where to begin, then it's time to find a coach or trainer. If you want to open that corner bar, talk to the owner of a corner bar!

We get stuck thinking that lessons are for kids. We drive them from piano to soccer, to gymnastics, football, and tutoring all because we recognize the importance of practice and coaching…for *them*! We often fail to transfer that same very useful principle to ourselves! WHY!? If we recognize the importance of coaching to learn a new skill, why wouldn't we adopt that for our own lives? When did we stop wanting to learn?

Here are a two things your new coach needs to demonstrate: They need to be successful in what you're pursuing. There are a lot of people out there who have strong opinions and love telling others what to do. If they haven't done it themselves, then I wouldn't trust them to truly recognize and know how to troubleshoot the obstacles that are inevitably coming. You need someone who's been there, done that, and won't be surprised by anything! You need to find someone who's kicking ass! The second thing they need to demonstrate is a belief in you. If they are arrogant enough to believe that their success is due to their own innate ability, or that they're more awesome than everyone else, then they can't coach you because they don't think you can do what they did. If you find that kind of a coach, a middle finger on your way out the door may be warranted.

Once you find this amazing, kick-ass coach who is excited for your dream and believes it with you, you are going to do everything they tell you to do. Period. When I'm interviewing a prospective client or partner, I ask them, "Are you coachable?" I go on to explain what I mean, "See, I believe you can kick ass at life even harder than me, and I know how to get you there. But if I give you an assignment, and you don't do it, then I'm wasting my time. So when you're ready to put on blinders, ignore your fear, give a stronger voice to your coach than to your critic, and take action, you will be blown away by your own achievement." I unfortunately come across a lot of potential clients who have exciting destinations in mind; I can offer them an amazing vehicle and teach them how to operate it; but their lack of confidence in themselves as a driver will derail even the best effort.

It's okay if you don't know how to get where you want to go, because someone else does. And maybe you don't even know where you want to go, you just know you're unsatisfied where you are. That's okay too. You're just going to pick something exciting and pursue it. The intentional pursuit of something exciting all by itself will get you out of your comfort zone and into the "World of Exciting Things" where you'll be surrounded by other people who are pursuing exciting things. And just by entering this world, you'll position yourself to become aware of all the amazing things out there to pursue! What you start pursuing may not be what you end up kicking ass at, but if you wait around in your comfort zone, fear and insecurity will likely blind you from anything new or exciting, until you're down the road and you haven't pursued anything.

The third reason we fail to take action is because we're too proud to start small. We're waiting around for the big stage, the big opportunity, the lights/camera/action moment. And until that opportunity shows up, we'll sit it out. A lot of people would love the opportunity to own a company with the prestige of Apple, but few are willing to start in the garage that they did.

I met Jimmy once at a park in Philadelphia. We were there with a group of guys to play a pick up football game. This was one of those niche group nerdy meet-ups. None of us had ever met in person before, but we all knew each other from the Philadelphia Eagles blog site that we spent way too much time interacting with.

We happened to meet outside on the coldest day ever in the history of days. It was the kind of day that makes you think global warming sounds awesome! While none of us could feel our extremities, it was still fun meeting people that we felt like we already knew. We loved putting faces to names, and putting real names to the pseudonyms we had become so familiar with online. This is the same kind of fun any hobby or fan group experiences when they get a chance to meet in person. It happened to be a bunch of Eagles fans playing football together, but the fun we had was the same kind of fun your Great Aunt Sally had with the knitting club last month at Ponderosa.

Jimmy was like the rest of us: Corporate guy, 9 to 5 guy, family man, Eagles fan. He was in the middle of all the conversations of the day:

"The Eagles are awesome!"

"My job sucks!"

"Wouldn't it be great if we could work for the Eagles, and get to see all their games, and it could be like, our actual job?"

"Yeah, that sounds great!"

"I mean, it'd never actually happen, the chances are so small. I wouldn't even know where to start."

We didn't play football long, opting instead to move to a bar where we could drink beer and feel our fingers. After some manly chest-bumps, a few farts that got blamed on the guys next to us, and some good IPAs later, we went back to our regularly scheduled lives and back to interacting on the blog site.

Jimmy went back to his 9 to 5, and like the rest of us, continued to write about the Eagles. But when Jimmy wrote about the Eagles, he actually invested time, energy and thought, as opposed to the angry and emotional rants the rest of us were throwing out there. His content got our attention, and very quickly we started using Jimmy's articles as the start of the conversation that would continue in the comments below it.

The buzz around Jimmy's writing also got the attention of the site's managers, and he was promoted to the thankless position of "Editor" which likely came with no perks and no money, but a title that nonetheless felt perfectly fitting.

But something else happened. The traffic and membership of the site started exploding, until traditional media outlets were forced to recognize its influence. Jimmy was quickly asked to contribute a guest piece to one of the local papers, and the feedback from that single article, led to a role as a regular contributor!

His style was refreshing, honest, and genuinely good! It wasn't long before that regular contributor role turned into offers from multiple publications competing for his full time service. Jimmy now writes full-time about the Eagles. He travels with the team. He's paid to attend every game. He has access to the facility. He talks with the players. Within 3 years from that meet-up football game, Jimmy was living the life that every one of us had considered a dream.

The only difference between Jimmy and the rest of the guys was that he just did it. He wanted to write about the Eagles, so he started writing. He didn't only want it. He didn't just dream about it. He didn't just complain about his job, wishing he got to do something much cooler. He started

> A lot of people dream about the big stage where they're recognized for their expertise, and celebrated for their accomplishments, but they aren't willing to get on the small stage and do the dirty work that actually makes them an expert!

doing what he wanted to do. He took action. But he took action on a small stage. He didn't sit around waiting for a major publication to come knocking on his door. He wasn't too proud to start small.

A lot of people dream about the big stage where they're recognized and for their expertise, and celebrated for their accomplishments, but they aren't willing to get on the small stage and do the dirty work that actually makes them an expert! We dream of being a best selling author, but we haven't written anything: not an article, not a blog, nothing. We dream of being a lead guitarist, but we can't play more than 4 chords, and we never find the time to practice. We want to be a celebrity chef, and while we might have the chef part down, we've never put ourselves out there in any capacity to be recognized as a celebrity. If you have a dream you just have to start. Start right where you are and start with the knowledge you have. Apple began in a garage. Wal-Mart was a single-location mom-and-pop retailer. Disney started in a shed. Starbucks began in Seattle by just selling roasted coffee beans that customers would brew at home. The only coffee they served on site were free samples. Just start! You'll learn as you go, and you'll never know everything anyway. Take what you do know, and just start!

Too often we allow analysis paralysis to indefinitely delay our start. This occurs when we're insecure in ourselves as drivers, but we fool ourselves into thinking that our confidence will grow as our competence grows. So we set out to learn everything we can about the vehicle.. We read every book. We read every blog. We memorize the look and language of successful people. We study the vehicle manual until we can recite it by heart, and we still don't actually put one foot in front of the other. If the driver isn't confident, they can know the vehicle manual and still be too insecure to turn the vehicle on.

Those same three years passed for all of the guys at that football game. Every single one of them wished to be where Jimmy was, and there's no reason they couldn't have been. Jimmy wasn't a better writer. He wasn't smarter. He didn't have more time or money. He had the same resources we all had. He just did it. He took action on the small, insignificant stage that nobody believed would ever matter or amount to anything. He honed his craft where it didn't matter, so he was prepared for when it did.

I do a lot of coaching on helping people develop their personal brand. This is a novel concept for many people. Most people don't think of themselves as having a brand, but we all do. And it's only the people who realize it who are positioned to develop it intentionally. When we think of a *brand*, we often lock our mind into the box of recognized companies: Applebee's, Bose, Southwest, Yeti, Lexus, Coke, etc.

And as I even mention those companies, thoughts are popping up in your head that you don't even control: reliable, innovative, fun, indestructible, luxury, etc. Sometimes the words you associate with a brand aren't good words. Maybe you hear a brand and you think things like: unreliable, dishonest, overrated, capitalizes on low-wage employment, greedy, cheap, poor customer service, etc.

If you've watched Simon Sinek's TED Talk titled "Start with Why," you'll realize that Apple has spent a phenomenal amount of marketing capital on sharing their story. As consumers connect with Apple, their core values, and why they're in business, that loyalty follows them regardless of what they choose to do. It's the reason Apple can launch an MP3 player, no different than other MP3 players on the market, but their iPod creates an entire revolution. It's why it has taken a decade for other electronic manufacturers to catch up and even rival Apple in mobile phone sales.

Apple worked hard to create a brand that people believed in, and that consumers were loyal to. They created a brand that made people believe: "I'm with them. Whatever they do, I want it, because I will be better for it."

The haunting question in all of this becomes: Which words pop into peoples' minds when they hear your name or think about *you*? Do people say about you: "I'm with her. Whatever she does, I want to be a part of it because I will be better for it!"? We have a brand. Each and every one of us has a personal brand, and for better or for worse the power of that brand is translated by the words that are conjured up in people's minds when they think of us.

What is your brand communicating about you? Does it say things like: "Always on time, works hard with enthusiasm, cares about others, infectiously positive, faithful in the little things, ambitious, happy, excellent, someone I would like to employ, or partner with, or even just grab an afternoon beer with"? Or does it say things like: "acts entitled, whines about what they don't have, always glum, rarely on time, does the minimum required, cares more about themselves than they do about others, someone I don't want to employ, I don't want to partner with, and I would need like 8 beers to even tolerate a conversation with"?

If you're uncertain about what your brand is communicating, look at your Facebook profile page, or your last 30 Insta posts, or the text conversations you're having. Do you find that you're celebrating the good in the world, or lamenting everything that sucks? Do you find that your public profile is fun, funny, informative, motivating, and exciting? Or do you come across like a sad, boring, and demeaning person who's constantly complaining, using foul language, and can't find anyone or anything good? It amazes me how many people complain about not getting the job, not finding people to help, or not having friends when they mope around like Eeyore from Winnie the Pooh whining about their lost tail.

Jimmy created a brand that communicated: passionate, great writer, funny, informative, exciting, attractive, inspires interaction. He did that on such a small stage that no one thought it was of any significance. He was simply himself. Even on a small stage that didn't matter; he was authentic. He wasn't trying to be anything he wasn't. He was passionate, he was a great writer, he was funny and informative, his pieces were attractive, and he inspired interaction. Because he showed that on a small stage where no one of significance was watching, he proved his character. He wasn't showing off, and that character was the reason the bigger stage opened up to him.

We're social people. We can't kick ass at life all by ourselves. It just isn't fun or fulfilling or meaningful. Seriously. What good is a giant house on the beach without an amazing pig roast and a live steel drum band with 30 of your best friends making a memory that will last a lifetime? What good is that amazing bottle of red without the laughter of a new inside joke shared between lovers? What good is achieving that amazing goal if you're celebrating alone? We need others, not just to enjoy our success, but to join us along the journey.

We need people because we need to be noticed and recognized in order for opportunities to open up. We need to build relationships to get favorable purchasing terms. We need to inspire loyalty to have a staff that works hard even when we're not around. Your brand is your reputation and it determines whether those doors open or not.

A lot of people don't take action because they're too proud to start on the small stage. You have a big stage waiting for you. You're going to inspire people with your weight-loss story. You're going to reach the top of your company and help coach young executives to do the same. You're going to open a business and inspire entrepreneurs from all over! You're going to have fan letters pouring in from your cook book, and it's going to be awesome! That might sound scary, or exciting, or terrifying, or amazing, or all of it at once. The thought of huge success might make you want to vomit, laugh, cry, and dance all at the same time. But you don't need to be scared, because it won't come until you're ready. You'll have to prove yourself on the small stage, where the lights are dim and nobody's watching before you can even audition for the large one. By the time you're on the big stage, you'll be ready for it.

Start preparing yourself for it now by taking action! Don't wait until you arrive on the big stage to start being the type of person who is on the big stage, because guess what? You'll be waiting a long time. Don't wait until you feel "#blessed"before you start recognizing that you already are blessed and acting like it. Your brand will determine your opportunity. So take action toward your goal with a brand that will attract the opportunity you want coming your way!

Step I is simple:

"Want something."

Step II is simple:

"Believe you *can* achieve what you want"

Step III is simple:

"Believe you are *worthy* of achieving what

you want"

Step IV is simple:

"Believe you *will* achieve what you want"

Step V is simple:

"Take back your story"

Step VI is simple:

"Take action"

Post Chapter Questionnaire:

Question 1: What has been holding you up from achieving what you want? If you haven't started, why not? If starting and quitting is a common practice, why?

Question 2: Where are you spending your time? Often we feel busy, but it's just a feeling that isn't backed up by facts at all. Sometimes looking at objective data can help us recognize things we wouldn't on our own. Make a list of the 3 most important things to you. Determine what it would take to achieve those things, and get those activities on your calendar first. Steven Covey in his landmark "Seven Habits of Highly Effective People" trains on how we shouldn't be prioritizing our schedules, because often our schedules are full of crap that isn't even important to us. We should instead be scheduling our priorities so that the things that are most important to us are getting done!

Question 3: Do you know someone who has done what it is you want to do? Your job is to endear yourself to them, so that you can become an apprentice and learn what it took!

Question 4: Looking at your social media account(s), what is your brand saying about you? Are you coming across like the kind of person who's successful at what you're starting?

Question 5: Is there an opportunity to start doing what you want to do? No matter how small the stage, is there a place where you can start, so that you can practice and hone your craft? If you want to write, can you start a blog? If you want to open a bakery, can you start having bake sales? If you want to be a designer is there a platform you can start promoting your design ideas? Where can you start?

Chapter VII:

#TheLongHaul

"We are what we repeatedly do. Success is not an action, but a habit." - Aristotle, ancient Greek Philosopher, scientist, one of the founders of Western thought.

"You'll never change your life until you change something you do daily. The secret of your success is found in your daily routine." -John C. Maxwell, American author and pastor, pre-eminent expert in business and leadership.

Taking action by actually starting is a necessary step that a lot of people don't ever take. We talked about this in the last chapter. But there's a temptation that can derail even the best of us once we do actually start. That temptation is very simply called "impatience." We overlook the fact that it took our entire lives to create the reality that we're unsatisfied with. We see where we want to go, and we want to get there right now! So what do we do? We take massive action. We cannonball into the deep end and swim as hard as we can! Then, 45 seconds later, when we're sweating even in the cold water and struggling to breathe, we realize, "Holy crap! I am way too out of shape for this! What was I thinking? I can't even breathe. My thighs are chafing. Is Grey's Anatomy new tonight?" And just as fast as we jumped in- we're right back to where we started with nothing but another notch on our "failed attempt belt" to show for it. This is, again, another example of stacking a destination on a foundation that wasn't strong enough to support it.

For some of us, it's not the "taking action" part that's difficult. At the start, we're often inspired and excited to take action! You want to lose weight, so you cut all carbs out of your diet, limit your calories to 800 a day, go to the gym for 5 hours, and fasten motivating pictures to your refrigerator. You have a great book idea, so you pitch it to a bunch a friends, sit down to write, and two weeks later, the cursor is blinking on a half-written page while you're watching cat videos on YouTube.

When we start something, we're largely dependent on excitement for motivation, but excitement can only carry us so far. If excitement is our motivator, at the first sign of things not being exciting any longer, we bail. The first obstacles that we face, totally derail us. Our friends' negative or even lukewarm reception to our business idea, is often enough to take away our excitement, and *poof*· There goes our inspiration to act. The minute we realize we're not seeing the results we expected or hoped for, we start thinking that our effort isn't worth it.

If we're going to move from idea to reality, if we're going to move toward making our dreams real, we're going to need to take steps after the excitement is long gone. Turning an idea into reality requires steady action, day in and day out. It sounds exhausting, but in reality, it isn't. What we call "reality" in our lives everyday, what we see as "real" — such as our weight, our relationships, our finances, our businesses, etc, — these aren't the result of what we want or dream of. They're not the result of the emotion we feel, or even the action we once took. Our realities, in all facets of our lives, are the carefully constructed result of the habits we've established and maintained with devotion.

The girl who's flawlessly fit didn't get that way because she decided to jog one afternoon and chose a salad for lunch that day. She's established healthy eating and activity habits that have delivered those results over time. Contrast with the guy who's out of shape: He didn't get that way because one day he ate a cheeseburger with extra fries and drank a 6-pack of beer. He's been on a negative trajectory for the last 11 years, having developed habits that are driving the results he's now seeing.

The couple with a large bank account didn't win the lottery. They prioritized debt reduction and saving, and the habits that they developed drove the results that they now enjoy. This is true in all of our lives. The couple in massive debt didn't get there because they got robbed. They developed a habit of overspending their income, and that habit drove the results they now live with.

Our realities are not random circumstance. Our realities are the natural consequences of the habits we do day in and day out, often without even thinking about them. Do you drive the same route to work everyday? It becomes mindless. Cruising down the road, you're not thinking of your next turn, you're thinking about anything and everything else. You've done this trip so many times that you're now on autopilot, and without any conscious effort you arrive at your destination with virtually no memory of the drive there.

We often don't even realize this until we're headed to the park on a Saturday and the route to the park overlaps our normal route to work. What happens? We totally miss the park exit, because mindlessly, we were heading where we always do. That's the power of habit. Habit drives results all the time, and it isn't exhausting; it's actually mindlessly easy!

The results in your life that you're now choosing to reject can only be changed when you realize that you brought yourself there. Until you take responsibility for everything, then you are simply a victim of your circumstances, and as long as your circumstances are bigger and stronger than you, then you are powerless to fight against them.

Look at where your business is. Look at where your physical body is. Look at where your relationships are. A long time ago, you made the effort and choice to take an action. Maybe you chose challenge, maybe you chose comfort, but you made a choice. And the next day you made the same choice, and again, and again, and again. Until that simple choice became so habitual you don't even think about it anymore. You developed a habit. The consequence of that habit is now the reality you live.

This should all be incredibly exciting to you because if you did it, you can un-do it. People worry all the time about whether or not they can actually be successful, and that's the most ridiculously insecure fear in the whole world! You've already proven that you can take action- develop a habit, and drive results. Granted, maybe the results aren't what you want. Sure, maybe the habits are driving you down a terrible trajectory. However, you proved that you can establish habits and drive results! You are already successful! All we have to do now is be intentional to replace our bad habits with positive actions. And we have to keep doing those actions until they become our new habits, driving us to new, and awesome, results.

And while it sounds easy, we have to resist the temptation to give in to impatience and move forward at an unsustainable pace. Here's a diagram to prove the point:

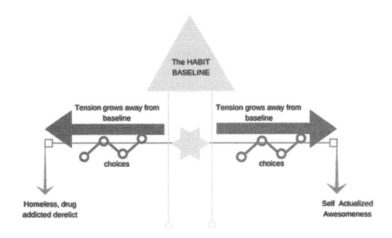

Life has what I call a "Reality Spectrum." All the way to the left is the version of ourselves that is a homeless, drug-addicted derelict, sleeping in a shed that the owner may or may not know we occupy. All the way to the right is self-actualized awesomeness where we have achieved the fullness of our potential in every area of our lives. And while either of those extremes exist within our realm of conceptualization, the reality we experience will usually be somewhere in between. In the diagram, our reality is indicated by the star in the middle. Your star may be a little more to the right, or a little more to the left in reality, but for illustrative purposes, I placed it right in the middle.

When we become unhappy with the location of our star, we want to move it to the right, closer to "self-actualized awesomeness," but the star can't just move because we want it to. It's locked into the frame of the "habit baseline". This is simply recognizing that our reality is driven by our habits. Inside the "habit baseline" are all the choices we make that are perfectly within our comfort zones. Think of those things you so easily do, like coming home from work and pouring that drink, waking up early and jogging for 30 minutes, saying words of affirmation in the bathroom shower, giving our spouse our full attention when they're talking to us, etc. These are all things we do with zero thought whatsoever. We do them everyday we don't even think about them. And the consequences of these habits have determined our reality.

If we're going to move the star, we need to develop new habits! New habits can't just happen. Habits develop from consciously making the same choice or performing the same action repeatedly until it becomes mindless. You cannot do anything new mindlessly, because it's new. New action requires thought. While you drive to work on autopilot now, think of your first day doing it. You pulled the route up on MapQuest, you researched the amount of traffic you'd experience, you likely test drove it the week before to time yourself, you checked out alternate routes in case you ever needed them, etc. There was nothing mindless about the first time, it was intentionally chosen.

To change our habits, we need to make intentional choices. If those choices and actions are going to become habitual though, they need to be simple and easy. This is where our impatience often derails us. When you make the conscious choice to perform an action outside the habit baseline, it requires thought and effort. The further that choice is from your baseline, the more thought and effort it requires, and naturally, the more tension there is.

If you are habitually waking up at 8:30 in the morning, and you decide that the "NEW YOU" is going to wake up at 5 a.m., that is very far from your habit baseline, and there is a lot of tension in that choice. If you choose, instead, to start waking up at 8 a.m., you are making a decision much closer to your existing habit, and there is far less tension. The farther that choice is from the baseline, the more tension there is. And that tension is true for choices to the left or the right of our baseline.

My friend Jamie has been a vegan for 15 years. For her to eat hummus and pita chips or a salad with oil and vinegar is simple and mindless. When I go out to eat with Jamie, her menu doesn't even open to the burger options. For her, the choice to eat a burger is so far from her habit baseline, the tension is so great, it becomes absurd to even consider. My friend Sarah has never done a drug in her life, except for alcohol, caffeine, and probably Tylenol. For her, the decision to shoot up with heroin would require so much tension as it's so far from her habit baseline that it's absurd to even imagine!

For a lot of us the choice to complete an Ironman Triathlon is so far from our baseline, it's not even a consideration. For some of us there's great tension in choosing to extend grace to our spouse instead of blowing off steam in their direction. When we get impatient for our star to move to the right, we often make choices that are so far from our habit baseline that the tension becomes exhausting to manage.

We can try to manage the tension and muscle up for a few weeks. We may even see some results, but then life happens: vacation, kids home from school, we get sick, we travel...and SNAP goes the tension and we fall right back to our baseline, having lost all progress! This is Bob's story with smoking. This has largely been my story with dieting. And I've seen this story play out so many times in business coaching calls. When we're driven by the initial excitement of our potential new reality, we summon the strength to manage the tension. But we cannot sustain that level of effort, and we inevitably crash right back to our old habits.

If you want a new reality you have to develop new habits. If you want to develop new habits you need to take new action, but, the action needs to be simple, easy, and intentional. Knowing where you want to go, you can choose an action that will get you there, or find a coach who can offer you a vehicle. The easiest thing is to choose a simple action that can fit into your day no matter what you come across. Jeff Olson, in his seminal book on habit development, *The Slight Edge*, describes the fact that he works out for 35 minutes every day. People ask him why 35 minutes. It's so specific. His answer is that if he scheduled a 45-minute workout, there would be days where he might not have 45 minutes, and he would make excuses and not do it. For him, 35 minutes fits perfectly because he can always find 35 minutes.

What simple action can you take toward your goal no matter what the day throws at you? What simple action can you do whether the kids are home or at school? What choice can you make whether you're working remotely or going into the office? If we can take an action that doesn't depend on our circumstances, then we can develop a trajectory that keeps us moving no matter what's going on around us!

Jeff understands that the game of success is about the long haul and not the emotional burst. He understands that the people who are going to kick ass are the ones that are still going strong 1 year, 5 years, and 10 years later. So when you're choosing your new action, choose one that you can do everyday for the next 10 years with no excuses. In order to do that, it better be simple!

To give another lesson: Whatever you choose to do gets easier. When you finally wrestle the kids to bed, you face a crossroad between comfort and challenge. You can choose to plop on the couch and grab a giant bowl of ice cream overflowing with whipped cream, or you can choose to grab a big glass of water and pound out 30 minutes on the elliptical. Neither of these is particularly hard. Having a baby without anesthesia is hard (and I've been corrected to note that having a baby even with anesthesia is hard). Quitting heroin is hard. Beating cancer is hard. You can watch *Desperate Housewives* on an elliptical for 30 minutes. That's not hard.

And the profound part of that choice is that whichever one you choose gets easier the next time. If you chose the ice cream, the next day, you're gonna get the kids to bed (FINALLY!), and you're going to remember how good that cookie dough was. How it totally "hit the spot." It was so nice yesterday that you'd really like to re-live that moment, and you'll go do it again. And then again, and again, until you're 2 months down the road and you're having to write "Ice Cream" as a line item in your budget.

But, if you choose the elliptical, the next day, it's easier to choose that again also. You'll remember how satisfying it was to do something intentional. You'll realize that you did it and you didn't die. It actually wasn't that hard. And you'll do it again. And then again, and then again, until you're 2 months down the road and you're having to shop for new pants because you can't keep your current ones up anymore.

It's imperative to be patient when wanting to change your life, and kick ass. We live in a microwave society that wants everything now, and that temptation to be impatient is both real and perilous! The best way I can recommend being patient and establishing habits that will drive awesome results is to set activity-based goals instead of results-based goals.

Let's say you work in sales. You set a goal of selling 10 units in a month, and you do everything right. You're meeting decision makers, building relationships, making your calls, and you get to the end of the month and you sold 2 units. Because guess what? In sales, the decision isn't up to you. Then you get to the next month, and set the same goal of 10 units. You do everything right, get to the end of the month, and you've sold 3. How many months can you miss your goal without getting depressed, discouraged, disheartened, or frustrated? Now you live with stress and anxiety all month wondering if you've got what it takes.

I know, because I've been there! I learned to set activity-based goals and simply ignore the results! This is the power of trusting the vehicle. If you trust the vehicle and the process, you can withstand delayed gratification. If you don't trust the vehicle, and you aren't seeing results, you're going to bail. You'll jump to a new vehicle, and then a new one, and you'll go from plane to train to automobile, never making any progress. So instead of deciding that you want to sell 10 units in a month, determine the amount of work it would take to make that happen, and then chunk it up. If selling 10 units would usually require 100 calls and 12 meetings, you're only going to focus on that activity. You're not going to focus on the results of the activity. In a 4-week month, that's going to mean 25 calls and 3 meetings in a week.

If this is my situation, I'm going to set my calendar to make 5 calls per day, and schedule meetings on Mondays, Wednesdays, and Fridays. Now, all of a sudden, hitting my goal doesn't depend on anyone but me! I'm going to reach or not, and it only depends on my own work ethic. What I'm going to find, is that I will prove my ability to set goals and reach them! I'll create a culture of consistency and success where I expect to hit my goals. That positivity is a much stronger attitude platform than the stress and anxiety I used to carry. And each time I set a goal and hit it, I build my belief in myself to actually be successful!

And, because I control the activity, it's easier for me to schedule my time. So I can do the work, reach my goal, and walk away feeling completely satisfied. If my calculations were right, and I trust the vehicle, the results are going to come. If, over the course of a few months, the results aren't coming, I simply increase my pace. While there are lots of variables we cannot control in our quest to kick ass we can always control our pace!

This little hack is an amazing tool anytime you have a big goal, and slow progress has the potential to rob you of the excitement. If losing weight is what you want, don't set results-based goals. You might do everything right and not hit. Losing weight can be a tricky thing at times. Instead, find a program, plan or trainer that you believe in, set activity based goals, and hit it every single day! You'll hit your goals, you'll feel proud, you'll establish habits, and the results will come!

Now, taking action and setting a plan to do it every single day without excuse sounds great. But there are going to be days that we absolutely don't feel like it. We all have seasons where we are rockstar motivated and primed to tackle the world, and days where we don't even feel like "adulting". How can we move forward on the days that we don't feel like it?

The first job, as we've talked about, is to ensure that your action is simple and the effort is sustainable. There's a big difference between not finding the motivation to spend 8 hours cleaning out the garage, and not finding the motivation to take a 25-minute jog. Finding the motivation to do a big thing is rare; you need to boil the big thing down into small, easy steps. If you've already crossed that bridge, then you need to make sure you have an accountability partner. You will only hold yourself accountable for goals other people know about. If your dream is still a secret, and you're working quietly and alone, you are going to get weak fighting the doubts and demons in your head. You need backup!

Find one or two people who love you and believe in you. Don't just share with them your ultimate goal, share with them the daily activity that you are committing to. Have them text you, call you, or stop at your house. It would be awesome if this person was also committed to the same goal, but as long as they're committed to you, then they're okay.

Do simple things that delay gratification and remind you to take action. I have coached people to boil their business activity goals down to three simple steps. I had them turn these steps into questions, and set a daily reminder on their phone that turns around and asks them every evening: Did you do X, Y, and Z? And they aren't allowed to turn on the TV or open the wine until they can answer YES!

The beautiful part through this struggle of motivation and accountability is that it's temporary! The struggle doesn't last forever. As we are faithful to do the work. the results will come. As the results come, our motivation to do the work will build naturally. Eventually, the action will become a mindless habit that doesn't even require motivation. That habit will be driving new results and you will have moved your star! Some people say habits take 21 consistent days to develop, other studies say it takes 90 days. Your mileage may vary, but it will happen. You'll know when it does, because you'll find yourself doing amazing things that you could never have done before and you won't even have had to think about it.

You'll find yourself looking awesome as you try on two-piece bathing suits for a cruise vacation, eating salads and not even missing the greasy chili fries. You'll laugh as you realize you just mindlessly paid the entire credit card balance and put an extra $500 into your savings account without even thinking about the daily Starbucks latte you gave up long ago. You'll wonder why you feel so connected to your spouse as you share a bottle of wine, look in each other's eyes, and talk excitedly about the future without even realizing neither of you has glanced at your phone for the last three and half hours. You'll wonder where the hot mess express went as you wake up at 5 a.m. easily, do your yoga, make kids' lunches, and sip coffee quietly alone in peace feeling grounded, balanced, and whole.

An awesome reality is waiting for you! You can take back your story, kick ass at life, and move your star. It isn't going to happen because you simply want it to. And it isn't going to happen by muscling up for a few weeks. And it isn't going to happen overnight. But it can, and it will happen. The only way to achieve those long term amazing results is not to make big choices that require a ton of effort and tension, but to make simple changes that gradually move your "habit baseline!"

If kicking ass were easy, everyone would be doing it. If everyone's doing it, then it isn't exceptional. But the secret is that while it isn't easy, it's also not hard! You simply have to be aware of pitfalls and intentional to combat them:

Pitfall 1: We don't take action because we don't know what we want. Pick something exciting and take action anyway. The pursuit of exciting things opens you to the pursuit of other exciting things and you will discover what you want along the journey.

Pitfall 2: We don't take action because we're scared. Use your rational mind to recognize the lies that you're inventing in your head. You get in your car everyday understanding that there is potential risk involved. You also understand that it's stupid to limit your potential based on unlikely consequences. So you drive on. Recognize the irrationality of your fear, and do it anyway. When it doesn't kill you, you'll be stronger.

Pitfall 3: We don't take action because we're insecure and unsure of our worthiness or ability to achieve great things. Realize that insecurity comes from believing the lie told by ourselves or our parents, or someone else that we're failures. When, in reality, every failure that we are acutely aware of came at the cost of achieving success somewhere else. Give yourself credit for what you have done instead of judging yourself or allowing others to judge you for what you haven't. Recognize that you are both already successful and worthy of greater success. Meditate on positive affirmations everyday, and surround yourself with people who believe in you and your dreams.

Pitfall 4: We don't take action because we have no idea what to actually do. Find someone who does know, endear yourself to them, and learn. You don't know anything until you know it. Don't stress not knowing, just learn it. This person should be kicking ass themselves, and they should believe that you can kick ass just like them! The best athletes, musicians, and CEOs in the world still all have coaches.

Pitfall 5: We don't take action because we're waiting around for a big opportunity. This is your pride. Shut it down. The big opportunity never comes until we've proven ourselves with the little things, and we've built a brand that attracts people and opportunity.

Pitfall 6: We take massive action and burn ourselves out before achieving long-term results. Slow down. Patience is the virtue here. It took your entire life to get to this point, it's going to take time to change it- so don't think you're going to do it overnight. Take inventory of your habits, and replace negative ones with simple, positive actions that you can do day in and day out without excuse.

Pitfall 7: We lose heart because the results aren't coming as quickly as we expected. If you didn't give in to

Pitfall 5, and the action you're taking is actually sustainable, then you simply need to shift your perspective from results to activity. Don't judge your success on your results (that are likely not even up to you), and instead judge your success on your activity (which is completely up to you).

By recognizing and avoiding these pitfalls, you will position yourself so far above your peers that your brand will become extraordinary, you will start toward your dream, refine what you want, learn how to pursue it, ignore the lies of insecurity, overcome your fear, not burn out quickly, and be primed for the long haul. You will find amazing opportunities coming your way and it isn't that they weren't available to you before, it's just that you never noticed them, or pursued them, or you gave up before they arrived.

WAKE UP, warrior! You've been drifting, and it's time to drive. You've been floating and it's time to fly. Your life has defaulted to auto-pilot because you were sleeping, and it's time to live a life by design instead of by default.

WAKE UP!!! There's an amazing life waiting for you, and it's time to kick ass, Green Ninja!

Step I is simple:

"Want something."

Step II is simple:

"Believe you *can* achieve what you want"

Step III is simple:

"Believe you are *worthy* of achieving what

you want"

Step IV is simple:

"Believe you *will* achieve what you want"

Step V is simple:

"Take back your story"

Step VI is simple:

"Take action"

Step VII is simple:

"Don't ever give up"

Post Chapter Questionnaire:

Question 1: What trajectory are your current habits promoting? Often we're not even aware of our habits, even though our realities are defined by them. We become aware by asking questions intentionally. What do you do when you first wake up? Which snack food do you automatically reach for? When you get the kids to bed, what do you find yourself automatically doing? As you ask these questions, you become aware of the habits you already have, and you can determine if they're good ones that are taking you where you want to go, or if they're bad ones leading you farther away.

Question 2: As you notice negative habits, what are some simple, positive actions that you can replace them with? Remember, if you're going to be successful for the long term-you have to take simple action. A lot of smokers find that getting rid of their cigarettes and placing packs of gum where their cigarettes used to be is helpful. Smoking is a ritualistic habit: wake up, light a cigarette; get in the car, light a cigarette. For a lot of people, it's not necessarily even the nicotine that they're addicted to, it's the ritual. Replacing cigarettes with a pack of gum allows the ritual of reaching for something and consuming it to continue. Be creative. What are some simple actions you can take — choose just 3 — to replace some of the bad habits?

Question 3: It's easy to get overwhelmed by big goals and feel so far away, or feel that progress is so slow we'll never get there. This is when we have to take our attention off the goal altogether, and focus on the activity. What can you do every single day — without excuse — that will bring the results over time? Can you set an alarm, or a reminder, or refuse to go to bed that day until it gets done?

Question 4: Who will hold you accountable to do what you've committed to do? You'll only push toward the goals other people know about, so it's important to put it out thoro. Your accountability partner needs to be someone committed to *you*. It's ideal if they have the same goals, mindset, and are committed to the same daily activity that you are, because you can work together and hold each other accountable, but that's not necessary. As long as they love you and are committed to you, then they can be a good partner for you. Find that person. Don't just tell them your goal, tell them what you're going to do about it every day. Ask them to be in touch daily while you're developing your new habit.

Credits:

Chapter 1:

Perry, Katy, and Bonnie McKee. "Roar." *Roar*. Katy Perry. Dr. Luke, Max Martin, Cirkut, 2013. MP3.

Tobak, Steve. "What Distinguishes Successful People? Less Than You Think" *Inc.com*, 10 June 2013, www.inc.com/ steve-tobak/what-distinguishes-successful-people-less-than-you-think.html.

Chapter 4:

Sincero, Jen. *You are a badass: how to stop doubting your greatness and start living an awesome life*. New York: Running Press, 2017.

Chapter 6:

Tony Robbins: I am not your guru. Directed by Joe Berlinger. Performed by Anthony Robbins. USA: Netflix, 2016. Documentary.

Maxwell, John C. .March 5, 2014. "John Maxwell on Leadership." The John Maxwell Company. Accessed January 16, 2018. http://www.johnmaxwell.com/blog/what-i-believe-about-success.

Sinek, Simon. "How great leaders inspire action." TED: Ideas worth spreading. Accessed January 16, 2018. https:// www.ted.com/talks/ simon_sinek_how_great_leaders_inspire_action.

Covey, Stephen R. *The 7 habits of highly effective people.* Selangor: PTS Publishing House, 2016.

Chapter 7:

Olson, Jeff, and J. M. Emmert. *The slight edge: little things matter.* Lake Dallas, TX: Success Books, 2009.

For more info on J&S Team Summit, Inc and to contact Jim,
visit our website: www.jsteamsummit.com